Executive's Guide to Effective Letters and Reports

Executive's Guide to
Effective Letters
and Reports

William M. Parr

PARKER PUBLISHING COMPANY, INC.   West Nyack, N.Y.

©1976 *by*

Parker Publishing Company, Inc.

West Nyack, N.Y.

Library of Congress Cataloging in Publication Data

Parr, William M
   Executive's guide to effective letters and reports.

   Includes index.
   1. Commercial correspondence. I. Title.
HF5726.P35   651.7'5   75-31910
ISBN 0-13-294165-1

*To Carol and Sandra, whose faith and
support inspired me to write this book*

What This Book Can Do for You

This book will be a most valuable tool for executives and others in business. It will save you precious time, effort, and money. This handy guide provides shortcuts to efficiency by giving proven techniques, as well as samples of actual letters that got the job done.

Chapter 7, for example, analyzes the critical area of sales letters, diagnosing the three distinct categories of this subject, as well as providing proven examples. Equally important are those letters that are written to rejuvenate old accounts and Chapter 8 explores the Seven Steps to Motivate Dormant Credit Accounts.

One of the most difficult and sensitive letters that you must write is the one asking for payment of overdue bills. Chapter 9 cuts right to the heart of this problem revealing the time-tested "Collection Series" letters, accompanied by a step-by-step analysis of these letters.

Chapter 11 gives you ten quick, easy steps to a better vocabulary that will arm you with the tools necessary to find and use the exact word for every situation. In addition, Chapter 12 includes a detailed guide to the proper use of the 60 most commonly misused words, plus a close look at 200 overused words with suitable alternatives.

Furthermore, this book shows you how to apply the magic formula that puts power into your writing. You learn how to use and remember the essential elements needed to achieve success and results through your writing efforts.

Now there will be a confident air to the letters and reports that you write, because you know they work. The fear and uncertainty will disappear and you will know that your writing will achieve its intended result, be it commanding attention, making sure it is read, winning the reader to your side, or making him respond.

By applying these tools and principles of solid, practical business writing, you will find that you will be saving hours and hours of valuable time. The time that formerly was needed to draft sales letters, adjustment letters, and the other forms of business correspondence can now be efficiently applied to the more demanding problems of your job.

The reason that you will be writing more confidently and saving time is because these are proven techniques used every day by those who write effectively. These techniques are easy to learn and apply because they are simple, clear and direct. I show you why a certain technique works and why something else doesn't.

The facts and principles advanced in this book are the result of more than thirty-five years in government and industry on the part of the author. This experience includes more than fifteen years spent in supervision and management, many successful years as an instructor, exhaustive detailed research and study, and an intensive interest in the subject.

This is a practical, down-to-earth book that will show you how to successfully apply the essential elements to significantly upgrade your writing skills. You will now have available one ready-reference guide to use in connection with whatever aspect of writing with which you may be involved.

William M. Parr

Contents

13. Researching the Business Report (cont.)

When Formal Report?
Key questions you should ask yourself before trying to write
Value and types of research
Three methods of gathering information
Completing your research

Executive's Guide to
Effective Letters and Reports

1

How to Apply the Magic Formula That Puts POWER Into Your Writing

"One of the greatest deficiencies we find in employees today is the lack of ability to express themselves well in writing. In fact, many of them shy away from doing it if they can find another way."

Such were the words of William F. James, Chief, Employee Development and Incentives Division of a large Department of Defense field activity, as he addressed a joint Government/Industry personnel training panel.

He further stated, "This should not be the case. If we could find a *magic formula* for converting that deficiency into an adequate, common, everyday skill, such as walking, talking, or driving a car, we could easily increase our efficiency 25-30% or perhaps even more!"

Just as surely as there are recipes for a delicate French cuisine, there is a magic formula for effective business writing. In fact, it applies to all forms of communication, either oral or written, and it's not hard to use or understand.

The formula can be stated in a very few words and just as easily remembered. If you would like to be able to write more successfully, quickly, and surely, simply be a *Speed Mason*!

"Hold everything!" you say. "I know what a brick mason is, or even a stone mason, but what's a *Speed Mason?*"

Obviously, a little explanation is in order here. Let's consider at first the definitions. A mason is "a skilled workman who builds with stone or similar material." Speed is defined as "the act or state of moving quickly, or to further the success of something." We can therefore state that a SPEED MASON is a person who builds, rather quickly and successfully, with strong material on a firm foundation to achieve a specific objective.

The objective in this case is to be able to write more successfully, in a reasonably rapid fashion, to our customers and business associates. I'm sure many people you know have made the observation that one of their biggest problems was lack of communication.

One of the biggest obstacles to good communication is not in what has been said, but in what has *not* been said. A learned authority once made the observation, "You must write not so that you can be understood, but so that you *cannot possibly be misunderstood.*"

It's an old truism: If you want to overcome or resolve a problem, first you have to *identify* the problem, and then take appropriate steps to correct it. This may well be true, but we have to reckon with a basic failure of human nature. Even though a person knows a problem exists, he either cannot or does not want to recognize the nature of it.

Many well educated people will not admit they are not good writers. As with many other things, the resolution of the problem has to start with the individual.

Possibly the biggest hurdle to overcome in the pursuit of truly effective communication is the wrong mental attitude of the writer. It is safe to say the great majority of people do not know what good letter writing requires.

Many well-informed executives will say, when asked, that good letter writing requires reasonably correct grammar and spelling as well as a good command of the English language. These are certainly necessary, but they are not the most important. More than anything else, good letter writing requires applied psychology or skill in the art of human relations. Secondly, it needs to use the *language that motivates.*

Success of any plan, mission, or idea can usually only result from effective communication. Good communication can only result from an *aroused* individual with an intense *desire* to create a better channel of understanding so he can *transfer* his belief to another person.

In addition to the definitions of the words as just described, SPEED MASON is an acronym I have designed to represent and help you remember the ten most essential *"how"* elements used to achieve successful communication. Without most of them, successful communication is impossible and, without successful communication, effective writing is also impossible. They are:

*S*oul	*M*otivation
*P*lanning and Preparation	*A*cceptability
*E*motional Stability	*S*implicity
*E*valuation	*O*rganization
*D*irection	*N*ovelty

Instead of trying to recall what ten items are essential to good writing and becoming confused, think of the term "SPEED MASON" and the elements will automatically spring into your consciousness. Not only will you be better prepared, but you will have a stronger feeling of self confidence by knowing you can remember and use them at will.

Put them all into use and you will, in almost every case, write well. At least, if you establish good communication, one of your biggest problems will have been resolved.

Admittedly, knowledge alone does not always insure achievement. Even knowledge, application, and hard work does not always produce results. Only if we know *how* or *why* something is done can we be reasonably sure of success.

The phrase "Be a *Speed Mason!*" is one short way of combining several factual elements into an easy-to-remember form and, by remembering it, we can put them to *use* more often and more effectively. Each facet of communication, be it oral or written, must recognize and properly utilize each of these elements.

Let's consider carefully the meaning behind each one:

SOUL

Most people will agree today that soul is important in the social and personal sense, even in the political sense, but they are not too quick to admit it has an important place in the truly business sense. I challenge that!

Maybe it is a cruel business world we live in. Maybe we should not expect the proper amount of consideration in our dealings with our business associates, but conditions are changing. Businessmen who have not been aware of or responsive to feelings and reactions of those with whom they have tried to communicate have long since paid the price.

A young securities salesman I know wrote a letter recently to a prospective client asking for an appointment. Two weeks passed without a reply from the gentleman, who owned a chain store. Then one day they met at a businessman's lunch. When they were introduced the chain store man said, "I hope you'll forgive me for not answering your letter. I'll be glad to have you come around and see me any time."

"Fine," said the securities man, pleased at the friendly invitation, "I wondered why you didn't answer."

"If you want to know the truth." the chain store owner explained, "your letter gave me the idea that you were pretty much of a stuffed shirt. Now that we've met, I realize you're a nice guy I'd be happy to talk to."

This young man discovered something that many people have learned in recent years—the letters we write can give a false picture of us. They can make us appear selfish instead of generous, pompous rather than personable, flippant when we mean to be friendly. For the recipients, the picture our letters paint is our personality, for better or worse. With care we can make our letters reveal the more attractive rather than the worse side of our nature.

Soul is the term used here because of what it is: the embracing of all understanding, human feeling, empathy, consideration for the needs and desires of other people. In many ways, we see only through our own eyes, or in a strictly subjective sense. It is the ordinary thing to do, the human thing, the easy way. A twentieth century philosopher has submitted that the major elements of SOUL are indicated by the letters of the word itself:

S incerity

O pen-mindedness

U nderstanding

L ove

There's nothing wrong with that. Do we have to be less tolerant, less patient, less understanding to prove we are a better person? That strikes me as being an anomaly. It seems pretty obvious that if we try to practice these elements in our daily lives, we would encourage others to do the same thing. The obvious result would be better communication.

Being human in the real sense (looking at a subject from the *reader's* point of view) creates a vehicle for better communication and will go a long way toward attaining our objectives. Taking heed of a person's problems, analyzing them, and giving the writer or reader the impression he is important to us brings about many benefits which create greater harmony, develop cooperation, and enable us to be much more effective.

In addition to developing greater understanding, it inspires confidence and trust, earns respect and generates more harmonious relationships. Moreover, it makes the reader feel important, encourages friendships, and produces more team work. Finally, and more important, it also helps to sell your ideas.

What are some of the tricks that words can play on us if we are not careful? Here's an example from a letter received the other day by a neighbor of mine who had asked two contractors for bids on a concrete driveway. One letter went like this:

Dear Mr. Dawson:

I am offering you a special price on this job because I am having a slack season just now, and my partner and I like to keep busy. I have some debts to pay and this work will be a big help to me. I would appreciate your patronage.

The first paragraph showed that the writer was suffering from a bad case of "I-me-itis." Not only the constant use of "I," "my," and "me," but the whole tone of the letter reveals the writer was thinking of *himself*, not of the person he was writing to. My neighbor's reaction was, "He sounds like a selfish kind of guy."

This man had violated the first rule of good letter writing: *Take the* **You** *attitude.* In other words, think of your reader's problems and forget about your own if you want to interest him.

The second contractor wrote as follows:

Dear Mr. Dawson:

I can give you a good, solid driveway with a 6-inch bed of cinders and 3 inches of concrete. Properly graded and drained, this could last you 10 to 20 years without cracking.

This man got the job because he told the customer what he wanted to know—what he would get, how he would be served, and what good it would do him—not how much good it would do the contractor to get the work.

It is surprising how many letters disclose, unknown to the writer, a suspicious, distrustful, antagonistic attitude toward the person to whom the letter is addressed. Somehow things we would never say to an individual face to face often creep into our correspondence.

So an all-important rule to follow is *Practice Courtesy*!

This means generous use in correspondence of "please," "thank you," "I'm glad," "I appreciate," etc. Words which rub the reader the wrong way—"We suspect," "You misunderstood," or "We can hardly believe"—are eliminated from the persuasive letter writer's vocabulary.

After these rules of letter writing have been mastered, there is still an undefinable quality or tone in a letter which comes from the personality of the writer. It can't be taught, but it can be learned. Maybe the following will show what I mean. It was written by the recently elected president of a large company to an associate of mine:

> Dear Ed:
>
> You are a generous and thoughtful friend as always to take the trouble to write me about my new job.
>
> I deeply appreciate your good wishes, to which I hope you may add a prayer or two. There are bound to be some occasions when I will need both.
>
> My thanks and only the best.
>
> Sincerely,
>
> Bill

Notice for one thing, this letter is extremetly informal. In the business and professional world today, dry, impersonal salutations, such as "Dear Sir" are rarely used. In writing to a stranger or someone we don't know well, we use the man's name, "Dear Mr. Randolph." Among personal or business friends, the first name or a nickname appears on most letters nowadays—the same name we'd use if we met the man on the street.

If you want to look at the other side of the coin, appreciating and understanding the other person's point of view counteracts, to a large degree, feelings of fear, hate, distrust, selfishness, greed, envy, jealousy, impatience, the urge to "get even," misinterpretations, indifference, and lack of motivation. My question is: Why run the risk?

PLANNING AND PREPARATION

If you can go into battle without being prepared and without fear, you must surely have been born with .45 caliber revolvers for hands. To do otherwise is pure folly. Why then do so many of us try to sell an idea or a product, get people to take action, or put across our point of view, without being properly prepared?

If we don't sell our idea or succeed in our efforts to win converts for what we want to do, then who can we really blame but ourselves? As they say: "We haven't done our homework."

Preparation, in the truest sense, covers several things—that is, preparation not only of the subject matter involved, but also of the *individual* we are addressing, as well as devising the proper *approach* to gain acceptance.

It is almost axiomatic that nothing fruitful or beneficial will occur unless you plan things out so that it will take place. More than likely, anthing beneficial that results without a plan is purely accidental.

This is a good time to bring up a problem or, should I say, the resolution of a problem that many people, principally supervisors, are faced with. The sad part of it is—they don't realize they have a problem. That problem, simply stated, is dictating a letter or a short report to a stenographer.

Much valuable time and effort is lost, in both Government and industry, because an individual does not dictate—preferring instead to write a letter out in longhand. The writer may consider it will be more accurate, concise, and complete if it is written out, but is it worth all the effort and, more important, is it really all that difficult to dictate to someone?

Many people have confided to me, "I never realized how easy it was until I got the hang of it." Don't put yourself down. Don't say to yourself, "It's too much trouble," or "It's easier for me to write it out." Give yourself a chance. Try it once.

Another fact you may have overlooked—your secretary is *supposed* to take shorthand. She would like to keep her "hand in," as it were. So you would be doing both of you a favor if you decided to give it a whirl.

Statisitcs show the average one page letter takes 42 minutes to develop, compose, and write in longhand. Assuming it took 10 to 12 minutes to get your material ready for dictation, it would take only two or three minutes to dictate. The whole letter would take less than half as long, and you would not have to write anything at all except, of course, some basic notes. Even if your secretary typed out your dictated notes in rough draft, you shouldn't have to spend more than two or three more minutes to edit. Then she could type final copy. Look at the time you would save!

The secret to being able to dictate effectively is merely being prepared for it. *You have to be prepared* to write, even though you do write it out yourself. So why not give your secretary a chance to help?

EMOTIONAL STABILITY

A veritable "bee in the bonnet," this element causes the most trouble and is the hardest to control. Many things are forever lost because we let an emotion, or maybe several of them, get in our way or take over our reason. This is more true of relationships with relatives than with business associates, of course, but it is still just as damaging to our interests.

Emotions can be of an infinite variety. It isn't just anger, hate, or envy. It can be greed, bias, prejudice, passion, infatuation, jealousy, false pride—any number of things. Emotion in its place (except where it destroys) is a desirable thing, but it will always cloud the way to clear thinking. The most unfortunate thing is in the fact that a great many people are guilty of having their decisions and their communications clouded by an emotion, or several of them.

This element is just as important on the other side (the reader) as it is to the writer. If the reader is angry, frustrated, or in a pallor of grief, the writer has a difficult task in trying to communicate with him. The reader's reasoning process is clouded with emotion. It would often pay dividends if you tried to determine whether your reader will be in the proper frame of mind when he gets your letter.

Let's suppose for a moment a Mr. Al Johnson had opened a charge account at your store several years ago and had been paying his bills on a timely basis until recently when, for some unknown reason, he stopped making payments.

You found out he owed $256.00 and had made no payments for the past three months. The bookkeeper has sent him a past due notice the first month and a form letter the second month with no results. You decided to "take the bull by the horns" and write him him the following letter:

Dear Mr. Johnson:

Our records indicate that you have owed us $256. for well over three months. We have written you about this matter several times before, but you failed to reply.

As explained to you when you opened your account, credit is only extended to customers who agree to repay their bills on a regular basis.

Therefore, we must ask for immediate payment of this bill in full. If you do not reply to this letter within 15 days, we will be forced to turn your account over to our attorney for appropriate action.

Very truly yours,

A.B. Samuels

What would you say the odds are on your getting payment of the overdue bill of $256.00? I would say your chances are (1) very small or (2) none at all.

You have undoubtedly satisfied your own exasperation over the apparent advantage a good customer has taken of you. But have you really accomplished anything? Have you considered any other possibilities, such as:

- Mr. Johnson is out of town?
- There may be illness or a death in the family?
- Mr. Johnson has suffered severe financial reverses and is ashamed to tell you about them?
- The customer has a complaint against the store and you are actually at fault?
- His payment was made but has been lost or misplaced?
- He has moved and his mail is not reaching him?

There are other ways to handle this particular problem, but the solution does not lie in issuing an ultimatum—at least, not before all other alternatives have been exhausted.

If you stop to think about it, emotional stability accomplishes quite a lot. It quiets an upset mind, inspires confidence, clears thought processes, and generally lowers blood pressure. You can help bring it about by being courteous, honest, tactful, patient, and thinking ahead to possible reactions to how you are going to express something.

An extremely hard person to communicate with is a person who has decided he is right and, when challenged, immediately adopts a "how dare you question my opinion?" attitude. Don't laugh—you might be guilty of this too.

A person who cannot admit he is wrong soon becomes a buck-passer. The two thing go together. Someone else has to be responsible.

Being wrong is certainly neither a disgrace nor a disaster, but refusing to admit that you are wrong can become one.

EVALUATION

Writing for a purpose without looking it over once in a while to see if it is going to do what you want, or has already done so, is like a chef cooking a dinner without testing it. It would be a huge gamble indeed to sit back and hope for the best.

Many people go about the business of trying to communicate with others everyday and never consider they might not be doing it properly or perhaps could do it better. They would probably say, "It's too much trouble to worry about it."

One good way to evaluate how well you are writing something is to try it out on a friend and to be *alert* to reactions on his part. He will show in many ways whether he is getting your message, or is even interested in it. If you are aware of these signs, you can and should make some changes.

One thing that should always be expected is the unexpected. No one can ever exactly anticipate what reception an idea will get. The reaction might even bring about improvements on the original idea over what you anticipated.

A frequent cause of lack of acceptance of an idea is not understanding the *language* used. One should always evaluate carefully whether the terminology being used is in the proper jargon or level of understanding of the listener or reader.

Anyone using a written form of communication can never be satisfied that it will always produce the desired results. Whether it is a direct mail campaign, procedural instructions, or group training, the results must be tested, measured, and revised to fit the needs of the moment. Only in this way can we be sure our message is going to get across the way we want it to and bring about satisfactory achievement of our objective. Nowhere is the old adage more appropriate: "Haste makes waste!"

I recently saw a memorandum from an executive in a large company which read, "If John Martin will see Jim Abbott and get the details, I'll talk to him later." Who was to be talked to in this case remained a mystery!

Examples like this lead us to another highly important rule in letter writing: *Say clearly what you mean!* When this rule is broken, it's often the result of hurrying. Before starting to write a letter, it is a good idea to think through what you want to say and the best way of saying it.

As added insurance, every letter you send out should be read over carefully before the envelope is sealed. When we use words that are confusing, in the wrong place, or with the wrong meaning, this tells the reader that we are careless and muddleheaded—qualities which inspire doubt rather than confidence.

DIRECTION

If a super businessman could analyze every failure of the past fifty years, chances are he would find most all of them were caused by lack of direction. According to E. Joseph Cossman, Mail-Order Millionaire, 92% of all business failures are due to lack of direction; direction at the top; direction down the line; direction whenever a crossroads is reached or a decision has to be made.

The *proper* direction at every turn will go far in assuring the success of any venture. This is equally as important in communication, for communication without direction is like an automobile running down the street without a driver. Everyone wants direction.

Look for a moment into your past. You have seen many an occasion when a little direction given by the proper party could have avoided a loss of prestige, a loss of business, or even a tragic consequence.

A simple example of lack of direction is seen in the following instruction:

"When the authorization form is received and validated with the Treasurer's letter, it will be forwarded to the Finance Unit."

What is to be forwarded—the form, the letter, or both?

Direction is important to everyone. It points the way, it helps someone to decide, it brings organization out of chaos, it shows priorities, it highlights important points, it identifies objectives and arranges them in logical order. It helps your reader to follow you down the path to the conclusion you want him to reach.

You would readily admit you can't follow an overall strategy, approach, or procedure unless someone has designed a plan and told you how to follow it through. Putting the shoe on the other foot, how could you expect someone to do what you want him to, unless you show him how or give him a clear written instruction to follow?

MOTIVATION

Motivation, not love, is what makes the world go 'round! If we are able, by whatever means we can employ to incite someone to act in our behalf, we have succeeded in *motivating* him. If we have not or cannot do it, for whatever reason, we have failed to motivate and, if we have failed to motivate, we have *failed* in our objective.

Many people still ask the question, "What really is motivation?" Reams of material and thousands of words have been written on the subject. The basic and perhaps best definition is the dictionary version, which says that motivation is "something that causes a person to act; an incentive, inducement, or a stimulus to action." Isn't this, after all, what we are trying to do when we communicate with others?

Motivation is not really a big word when we understand how it works, Boiled down to its barest essentials, *motivation* and *emotion* go hand in hand like ham and eggs, or shoes and socks.

Emotion is created by *verbal, live and active words, descriptive and sympathetic terms, or simple and exciting verbs.* So, too, is motivation to act. If you would stimulate anyone to action, look to your language. If it is dull and stodgy, devoid of action and, in most cases, long and drawn out, you will have trouble motivating even your best friend.

There are two ways to look at every situation—call them positive and negative, downbeat and upbeat, or simply gloomy and cheerful. Many writers reveal unwittingly their fears and doubts rather than the constructive ideas they want.

This leads up to another extremely important rule for good letter writing: *Accentuate the positive!*

For example, a large manufacturer of building materials found not long ago that a new type of asbestos shingle was not selling as well as an older style, although it was superior. A young man handling orders for the company wrote the following letter:

Dear Mr. Paine:

I am sorry to tell you that we no longer make the kind of shingles you inquired about. We have, however, a new style which may fit your needs.

This apologetic, negative approach was changed around by inverting the order of statements as well as the tone:

Dear Mr. Paine:

I am happy to send you samples of our new roofing shingle, which now comes in a wider range of colors and textures than before. It is a great improvement on the old style, which it has replaced.

Both letters told the truth, but the second one took a positive approach which made the reader *want to see* the new shingles, instead of making him *sorry* about the discontinuance of the old style. Sales in the department began to rise almost immediately.

Before leaving this subject, we perhaps should give you a fairly modern, time-tested technique for using Motivation to get your reader to respond the way you want him to. You might say it is actually four techniques in one:

1. *Put the reader in the picture* with proper use of the **You** attitude. To capture his interest and understanding, you must first capture his attention. What better way to do it than to talk about *his* interests?

2. *Appeal to the reader's emotion.* As stated earlier, people respond first with the heart, then with the mind. This, of course, requires a continuation of the **You** attitude.

3. *Convince the reader's mind.* Now that you have successfully insured your reader's attention, you can bring into play your facts and logic. Only now can you safely begin to use "we."

4. *Stimulate your reader to action,* still with a continuation of the "we" attitude. Show him **Why** it will pay to act *now.* Ask for the order, or show him why he will either gain by acting right away, or lose something of value if he fails to act.

If you practice this technique as you should, I can practically guarantee results.

ACCEPTABILITY

Communication frequently breaks down for one principal reason: Mental Rejection. For many psychological reasons, people resist the input of new ideas into their storehouse of knowledge. Primarily, it interferes with their normal routines or their established way of doing things.

The word *acceptable* covers many things. First of all, it includes or implies anything which is rational, fair or logical. Many times an idea is rejected because it does not meet this test, and the writer does not realize he has not made his point.

Until the writer puts together an idea or a concept which can be accepted, he is wasting his time covering the other points. In other words, he is not communicating with the reader.

Another facet of acceptability is that of "speaking the same language" as the reader. If the author is not using words, terminology, or jargon with which the reader is familiar, the latter will *reject* it because he doesn't understand it.

He may not perhaps realize he doesn't understand, or he may simply be afraid to show his ignorance and ask for clarification. He will just wait for something to come along he can accept. The fact that the writer has not in fact reached the reader may never come to light.

One of the biggest problems a writer will face is *misinterpretation*-that of assuming a meaning not intended. Rather than being acceptability in the strictest sense, we might call it a fault created by *over-acceptability*. The reader is always in a hurry to get the message, or accept the idea being expressed, especially if it agrees with his own. Thus, he frequently falls into the trap of getting the *wrong* message or idea completely.

Hundreds of words, perhaps even thousands, have *double* meanings. It is one of the pitfalls of the English language. The word "priceless" is one example. Does it mean "without price" and therefore cheap, or does it mean so high in value that money couldn't buy it?

More significant and perhaps a much greater problem than the double-meaning word is the use of a word *out of context*. This occurs when we use a word from our frame of reference, but it doesn't have the same meaning from someone else's frame of reference—words like rich, poor, hot, cold, dumb, smart, short, tall, old, new, etc.

For example, if a native of Arizona was to describe the weather of a certain location as cold, a native of Montana would probably scoff and say, "Why, that's shirt-sleeve weather in my home town!"

One of the best ways to avoid this problem in trying to get your message accross is to put yourself in your reader's shoes, or *think in his terms*. In other words, ask yourself, "What is his background, his level of understanding, what impression is he likely to get from what I say?"

If you give the proper amount of thought to this principle as often as you can *before* you write on a subject, you will go a long way in preventing a communication breakdown.

Still another measure of acceptability is whether something is *important* or *beneficial* to the reader. This is a continual process of evaluation on his part for, when he reaches a point in time of deciding that it is neither, he will "turn you off" mentally. This is why it is so important to make as favorable an impression as you can on your reader *before* you get down to the main issues.

One final thought on the subject. A strange things occurs when a thought, being transmitted in writing, is not *completely or properly expressed*. The mind of the reader says, "Whoops! That idea does not make sense at all; therefore, I will reject it completely!"

This is the reason people who have trouble either constructing or finishing a sentence also have a lot of trouble communicating. This problem more often than not creates an inferiority complex and makes these people less willing to communicate. This tends, of course, to compound the problem even further.

SIMPLICITY

Whatever happened to the simple life? Why is life so complicated? Is it because we consider it the fashionable thing to do? Are we afraid to say we don't really understand the complex and be thought uneducated, unsophisticated, or even inferior?

One of the hardest lessons for the average writer to learn is that everyone he writes to is not on the same level of understanding of the subject as he is. This is not to imply that the writer is superior or that the reader is inferior, but the writer has had to become well versed on the subject, else he could not transfer that knowledge to others.

This is another area where mental rejection plays a highly significant part. The mind of the reader says, "It's too complicated; I don't understand it; I won't accept it."

You obviously wouldn't preach physical theorems to a music student, even though the latter might have a high I.Q. The sad part of it is, if you do, your message has gone "over the head" of the reader, and there is no easy way to make you aware of it.

This brings us to another highly important guide to more effective letter writing: *Be Yourself!* The best letters are written as you would talk, in everyday language.

A recent Governement pamphlet campaigns for the same thing, which it labels "straightaway English." The authors point out that official jargon or "gobbledygook" wastes time, tax money, and storage space. The booklet recommends that long, stuffed-shirt expressions, such as "ameliorate," "compliance," and "enclosed please find" should be tossed in the wastebasket, and suggests bureaucratic letter writers stick to the simple things, like brevity and sincerity.

The businessman who uses such phrases as, "Yours of the 7th," "Agreeable to your communication," and "Receipt is acknowledged of . . ." gives the impression he is a pompous egotist who has no friendly feeling for the person he's writing to. If you want to tell someone you received his letter, why not say, "I received your letter and. . ."?

Another rule for good letter writing which closely parallels the previous one is: *Be thrifty with words!*

The other day I saw a letter which began like this: "Mr. Long has offered a suggestion regarding a departure from our standard procedure with respect to remuneration for overtime employment." I didn't go any farther, because I had to stop and figure out what all those words meant. If the writer has simply said, "Mr. Long suggested a new way to pay for overtime," I'd have been interested at once!

Simplicity (and that includes brevity, clarity, and conciseness) greatly enhances mental understanding, acceptance of an idea, maintains the reader's interest, makes objectives more plain and easier to achieve, and generally improves the learning situation.

The use of cartoons, diagrams, and photographs has proven many times the advantage of making things simple.

ORGANIZATION

Strange as it may seem, many people do things well, but they never seem to get organized. One would think none of the other elements mentioned above could be very effective at all if what you write is not properly organized.

The reason this element is so important to good communication and is specifically mentioned is the fact that the majority of people speak without thinking or sit down and write without getting all the necessary information together and arranging it in logical sequence.

Webster's Collegiate Dicationary defines the word *organize* as: "To arrange or form into a coherent unity or functioning whole . . . to arrange elements into a whole of interdependent parts."

To make any letter, report, procedure, or simple instruction have the effect you need or desire, it must be properly organized for the maximum impact, e.g., the "attention-getter" right on top, the next most important points near the top, etc. All the necessary items must be included, the unnecessary and extraneous must be excluded, and what is used should be so arranged to present your material in its most forceful light.

Much good material is often wasted in a long letter or a report simply because it was poorly or inefficiently organized. So, if you want to put your best foot forward, look to your organization!

NOVELTY

Why is this element so important? You ask, "Will it help me write a better letter?" It has been proven many times that the *most satisfactory* communication experience resulted from a *novel or different approach*. The reason for this is because the author *attracted attention* with it.

Most everyone knows the first and foremost action in getting a speaker's point across is to get the listener's attention. If he is successful, the speaker can proceed with reasonable assurance that his next point will at least be heard, whether it is understood or not.

If he is not successful, he might as well pack up and go home, for now he has nowhere else to go with his message. This is even more important in writing, because it is harder to hold someone's attention with the written word. For example:

Dear Mr. Chalmers:

We have just heard from Mr. Fran Ellison, who calls on you, about your wife's recent operation. We were indeed sorry . . .

Wouldn't you agree that Mr. Chalmers is going to take the time to read that letter? You bet he is! First of all, it shows effective use of the "You attitude."

In addition, Mr. Chalmers is undoubtedly interested in what you might say about his wife. Your concern also shows you to be the type of individual he can trust—or at least, it so appears. This is mainly because your interest in the reader is greater than your interest in yourself.

The novel approach doesn't have to be exciting, funny or dramatic to be different, but it should cause some *favorable reaction* on the part of the reader. Sometimes this approach can be equally effective by not being dramatic. Anything that amuses, shocks, makes an impression, or otherwise gains attention may be considered a successful opening.

The best way, perhaps, to find a novel beginning is to ask yourself, "What can I offer that is different?" You will be surprised, often times pleased, at what you come up with.

In summary, the ten elements we have outlined tie together to form adequate communication, and that means improved writing skill. None of these elements, good as they are, have any substance or meaning, unless they are properly conveyed to the reader.

Whether writing a simple letter or a report, or detailing complex procedures, you will be successful only to the degree that you give adequate consideration to these factors. If you consciously apply this Magic Formula, you will find it truly puts POWER into your writing.

2

Constructing Executive Letters that Command Attention and Get Results: The First Dimension

A letter speaks: "I am a letter! Take a minute to look at me! Here I am: a simple package for carrying a message. I am so characteristic in my apperance you know right away what I am. I have a head to show where I came from and when I left. An address tells my destination. The close helps you know who sent me. My body tells you why I'm here and maybe how I came. I add a salutation to say hello and a complimentary close to show the proper respect. Now, with all the help I'm giving you, you should show a little respect for me!"

It's a verity we can all appreciate. All the frills and formalities are already known or provided to us. Our only real problem then is the *body* of the letter—the message itself. This is where the action is. We need to channel our efforts and plan out our letter to do a job for us. Therefore, Strategy is the First Dimension.

Essentially, you have to do only four things:

1. Decide on your objective.

2. Put it down in clear and simple terms.

3. Be convincing.

4. Make it easy for your reader to agree with you.

Now, if it were all that simple, there would be no real need to write about it or study the problem. None of us can really afford to just collect all our facts and opinions in a basket and send them off like a bag of laundry in the mail to our correspondent.

Several years ago, a survey of business letters in several big companies showed the sad fact that only 42% of them were deemed acceptable by reasonable standards. Of the 58% that would *not* meet the test, 45% were too technical or full of company jargon. The remaining 55% consisted of follow up letters to clarify a previous letter, were simply lacking in tact or business etiquette, or made no sense at all. Is it any wonder the public gets upset over some of the letters it receives?

I am reminded of the words of K.M. Chrysler, who proclaimed about 20 years ago: "Our letters are often the first representatives our business friends meet. We should make them friendly, factual and helpful. We don't need creaky old phrases."

We all have many reasons for writing letters, not counting those we write to our relatives and friends. We can make them as long or as short as we like, formal or informal, inquisitive, informative, demanding, sarcastic, or even a combination of all. We can jump right in, get it "off our chest," and say what we want—or we can give a letter some judicious and careful planning. How ever we do it, we soon realize we will get results equal only to the thought and effort we put into the letter beforehand.

ORGANIZING TO WRITE

Organizing to write is the most important phase in the writing process. You can use your best college grammar; you can punctuate precisely according to the rules; you can construct smooth flowing sentences; but if you don't organize your writing logically and in a sequence that will lead your reader from one point to the next, you may as well not write at all.

Some sage once made the observation there were only three requirements for a good letter, i.e.,

1. Sound thinking;

2. A friendly attitude; and

3. Good expression.

In a broad sense, this is probably true, but I'm sure each one of us would like to have a little more specific guideline in order to improve our writing efforts. First of all, before you can hope to *write* clearly, you must first *think* clearly. You should systematically think through what you are going to write before you put anything on paper.

One of the best ways to organize to write is (1) to set up a more or less mechanical step-by-step procdure which will make it easy for you to follow, and (2) if followed, will automatically lead you to the end product—a well expressed thought on a well organized paper.

Let's say, for example, you were in charge of the Contract Department of Vance Electric Co., a small electrical manufacturing firm that had a good sized subcontract (VE-1207) with Alliance Products Co. which, in turn, had a prime contract with the U.S. Air Force.

Production personnel of the prime contractor had been inquiring quite frequently in the past few weeks about the delivery status of your subcontract, which called for the shipment of 100 Assembly Kits. The contract should have been delivered by the end of February, but you had not been able to furnish the items on schedule.

On March 3rd, Mr. Clark of Alliance Products wanted to know what was wrong and what you intended to do about the late delivery. Your investigation revealed you had received a revised delivery schedule from your Production Department with accompanying explanation covering the following:

- Company had encountered a production breakdown on the # 180-2 tube, major component, caused by inferior material supplied by a vendor.
- Tooling was not adequate, appropriate, or in conformance with specifications on:

#785 Retainer   #655 Rod
#1200 Clamp   #509 Adjusting Screw

- You were not getting necessary approvals for modifications in inspection tooling designs from the prime contractor, Alliance Products.

To resolve the problem, you needed an extension of the delivery schedule. To do this properly, you needed a change to the contract and you felt you should get this contract change at no cost.

How would you compose a letter to the prime contractor to achieve the foregoing objectives without being rambling or verbose?

Here we have, quite obviously, a good opportunity to exercise our ability to plan and organize before composing a letter. If we were to simply relate the foregoing, for instance, in straight chronological fashion, we would indeed lose our battle. We would probably end up paying some sort of damages for our inability to perform.

QUESTIONS YOU SHOULD ASK

The first question, therefore, is: How do we attack the problem? The best place to start is to ask: What do I want to *end up with*?

There are two answers to that question. No. 1 involves the *format* of the letter. No. 2 concerns the *objectives* we want to achieve by our letter.

As far as the letter is concerned, we can safely say the usual format of a business letter contains the "Basic Five:"

1. Opening—reason for the letter.

2. Preparation—set stage for the message.

3. Explain the details.

4. Motivation—ask for action.

5. Close.

Working within the framework of this format, the best approach to Question No. 2 is to study the problem and relate the specific nature of it to each part. In summary, we would proceed somewhat in this manner:

- Refer to inquiry (reason for letter).

- Show seriousness of the problem and your concern about it.

- Set stage for agreement of the addressee with your opinion as to your company's reliability and sincerity.

- Show that a complete job was done on the problem.

- Categorize reasons for the problem:

  1. Highlight problems (give #1 priority) caused by the other party or circumstances over which you had no control.

  2. Second priority—problems for which you perhaps were only partially responsible.

  3. Third priority—miscellaneous problems or problems for which you were wholly responsible. Group together in one category and de-emphasize them if you can. For greater impact, try not to give over three priorities of problems.

- Ask for what you want and tie it in with the explanation. If you want a concession by the other party (if not a major concession), try to treat it as an accepted fact or a logical conclusion.

- Use a cordial and business-like sign off.

After we have answered these questions and arranged our material, we are ready to compose our letter. The words we would use are varied and the reasons are many, but we should be able to keep the end result down to one page. One example of a resulting letter, using this technique, is shown in Figure 1.

INTRODUCING THE "FIVE-SIDED FORMULA"

Many years of research and painstaking analysis of business correspondence of all types by learned scholars has brought to light a technique which has proved very successful in preparing good letters. If you want to create a good letter, you would be well advised to try it.

The technique is called the "Five-Sided Formula." In essence, the formual specifies you must consider five points or, as I often prefer to call them, dimensions in preparing an effective business letter—a letter that will command attention and get results.

Figure 1

March 7, 19____

Alliance Products Co.
Attention: Mr. Edwin Clark

Dear Mr. Clark:

Your inquiry into the status of delivery of 100 each #205VEK Assembly Kits, on our contract #VE-1207, provoked my immediate and concerned attention. As you are well aware, we seldom experience delays in meeting our contractual commitments unless there is good cause. Therefore, I personally investigated into that cause.

A thorough study indicates to me the delay was indeed excusable. Three major reasons caused the delay:

a. Having to wait for approval of inspection tooling designs by Alliance engineers:

b. Production breakdown on the #180-2 Tube, brought about by inferior material supplied by a vendor; and

c. Minor production tooling discrepancies being resolved.

In view of the above, we recommend you issue a modification extending the contract delivery schedule for the kits to April 30, by which time these conditions should have been alleviated. We also recommend, since you have in effect received consideration for the extension due to the delays occasioned by your engineers, the modification be issued at no cost.

If you have any further questions about this matter, please call me. I will be glad to discuss it with you.

Sincerely,

Adam Smith

As mentioned earlier, nothing fruitful will occur unless you plan things out so you will have a reasonable assurance they will take place. Planning invloves consideration of three things: (1) your ultimate objective, (2) obstacles you may have to face, and (3) methods you might have to use to achieve that objective.

HANDLING THE FIRST DIMENSION

The First Dimension, therefore, must concern itself with the all-important question: How do I approach the problem and plan and organize the letter so as to maximize results? In other words, what should my *strategy* be?

Our first consideration is to determine what we want to accomplish; in other words, to decide on our objective. After we have decided this, the next question is: how best to go about it? Depending, of course, on the type and importance of the letter, this element often becomes the most important of all five elements. Everything else must ultimately follow.

The first ten or twelve words of a letter are the most important. Every writer must have a clear purpose. If he does not, his beginning is going to be weak and ineffectual.

Unless you're answering a routine request for information, or asking a simple question, you are trying to "sell" something or win someone over to your point of view. Therefore, you should find a "hook" to get the reader's attention. You may even want to start somewhere in the middle of the discussion, if it is more effective. This is often done.

A dramatic opener is always good. Tell the reader what he wants to know—as far as you can. For example:

Dear Mr. Jones:

We are pleased to inform you we are replacing your battery charger without any additional cost to you. Mr. Harper will bring it over to your office as soon as it arrives from the factory and pick up the one that has been causing difficulty.

We expect the new one to arrive early next week. You are due an apology for our not honoring the warranty agreement immediately, but our Service Department Manager was not aware of the particulars.

Please let us know if you encounter any more problems. You may be assured of prompt and careful attention.

Sincerely,

Tim Cole

You will note you are giving Mr. Jones the good news first—with the use of three magic words or phrases: "pleased to inform you . . .", "replacing . . .", and "without any additional cost. . ."

As mentioned before, the reader is an individual and is all important. *Get him on your side.* Be as specific as you can, but be believable. Use simple writing, but be persuasive. Remember, your greatest persuasiveness comes from talking from the *reader's* point of view!

To get yourself into the proper frame of mind, or mood, if you like, ask yourself certain pertinent questions:

- What kind of a fellow is the reader?
- What do I want the reader to do specifically and what facts will he need to know?
- What can I do to induce him to act?
- What objections might the reader raise?
- What is the best order of ideas? Facts?

To make your letters more attractive and readable, avoid setting up big paragraphs, or long, imposing blocks of type. They will almost always repel the reader. Break them up into two or three shorter ones, especially the *opening* paragraph.

Make your close work for you. Make the reader *act*, or leave him with a good impression. Do you want to insure a reply? Send a stamp or a self-addressed stamped envelope or, if you have one, a business reply envelope.

Unfortunately, there is also such a thing as giving a customer too much information. If you were to give, for example, a reader five or six alternatives to choose from, you would probably confuse him and get no response at all. Instead of giving him so many choices, reconsider your proposition and give him the two best or, at the most, three alternatives. You can tell him there are others if he is interested, but don't make his decision-making process too complicated.

When you have resolved the above questions, you are in a position to write a pretty good letter. One of the next problems that usually comes up is the question of length. Should you use long copy or short copy? The most correct answer to that question is: "usually short."

If your product or service is capable of delivering an important benefit, however, always provide your reader with *wanted* information. When you have said adequately what you think ought to be said, stop. Nevertheless, you should take a long, hard look at anything that's going over *one* page.

There are times, however, when a longer than average letter may be called for. For example:

1. A demand does not already exist for the product or service. Even this should be as brief as possible.
2. Your offer is hard to explain (perish forbid!).
3. The price is high (by reasonable standards).
4. The matter must be considered or taken up with others.
5. Reader is apt to be resistant.
6. Product bears directly on the reader's success or happiness.
7. Reader has shown a previous interest.

If your letter or reply does not qualify on any of these points then, by all means, it should be as short as possible.

THREE SIMPLE CATEGORIES FOR YOUR REPLIES

When answering a letter, most replies may be classified into one of three simple categories: Yes, No, or Maybe. If it is No or Maybe, you have a selling job on your hands. Consider your reply carefully and classify it into one of the three before preparing an answer. The following guidelines can help you determine which it should be:

Yes: Does it contain information which will please the reader?
No: Does it contain bad news?
Maybe: Does it contain a partial rejection or a request for action for which the reader is not prepared?

Category 1, **Yes**–Summarize the whole story in the first sentence and follow up with necessary details. You may, if you wish, end with a short "punch line" recalling the benefits of the good news. Letters which merely give information are in the same category (see Figure 2).

Figure 2

March 10, 19___

Calgary Products

Dear Mr. Gordon:

Your query was very timely. You asked if there was any way you could be assured of receiving immediate attention when your driver came over to pick up supplies from our warehouse.

We have alerted our staff to the effect that, when a Calgary truck arrives, a man from our Express Section will be assigned to assist your driver in filling your order and getting your material loaded expeditiously.

We have recently installed a program of giving small orders (less than 500 pounds), as well as our preferred customers, prompt attention. Since you have been a volume buyer and a good customer of ours for some time, we have included you in the latter category.

We are happy to be of service to you now and in the future. Your satisfaction and good will is important to us and our continued relationship will benefit us both.

Sincerely,

Joe Stevens

Category 2, **No**–The object here is to try to catch the reader's *favorable interest* in the opening sentence with something on which both reader and writer can *agree* (perhaps something customer has done for you). Then point out all the reasons why you can't do what he wants. To close, select some talking point of favorable interest which demonstrates your desire to retain him as a friend (see Figure 3). Some special rules for "No" letters:

- Give good news quickly and cheerfully.
- Conversely, pave the way for refusals by "getting in step with the reader" and give him a clear explanation before making the refusal.
- Be sparing with apologies.
- Use the "You" approach.

- Accentuate the positive.
- Don't be afraid of using the pronoun "I" if it helps.
- If you can say YES, say it at once; if you must say NO, take a little longer.

Figure 3

March 10, 19___

Palmer Tool Co.
Attention: Mr. J. Palmer

Dear John:

Your letter was received today and it certainly deserves my personal attention. As you know, we have been friends for many years and I sincerely intend to continue that relationship. We have done many favors for each other during the past and you have done business with our company for several years.

Your request for preferred treatment when your driver comes over to pick up supplies from our warehouse is certainly not out of order. I would like to oblige but I cannot, in all fairness, do so under current circumstances. Our Shipping Department is set up on a scheduled, planned priority system much the same as yours. I'm sure you will agree, for maxiumum efficiency, it must operate this way.

This does does not mean, John, you will not receive prompt attention and courteous service as always. Matter of fact, it should even be better than it has been. Adhering to this system allows us to function in an orderly and efficient manner and continue to provide you the necessary service to which you are entitled.

However, John, I will mention one thing. Whenever you are going to pick up less than 500 pounds, you are entitled to use our Express Section. There you will receive immediate service. This special department was recently established to expedite small LCL shipments and has proved very successful. This service should resolve most of your concern.

I'm sure you will understand and appreciate we have your interests at heart as we do all our customers. The procedures we have installed should work to everyone's benefit. Should you find, however, to the contrary, don't hesitate to call me.

Cordially,

Brad Myers

Category 3, **Maybe**:

1. Here you want to show *two* peaks of interest (the reader's and the writer's). Start off with something your reader wants to hear to catch his interest and try to maintain it. Not until you have *fully* developed the benefits are you in a psychological position to ask him to do what you want.

2. When you close a letter, make it clear why it is to the *reader's* interest to do what you want. Keep *yourself* and *your* wants out of the close.

3. Don't insult your reader's intelligence with the time-worn phrase "Do it Now!" He will resent it. Make him *want* to take the proper action.

4. The "hurry up" or urge to action, should be a limit in time, or a limit in quantity, or both. It should be a plausible reason why the reader must act without delay. It should *give* him something if he acts right away and *take away* something if he doesn't.

5. Prove your case! It should be more than merely your assertion that the buyer will benefit, and it should be spread through the whole letter, not just tacked on at the end as an afterthought (see Figure 4).

Let's take a moment to analyze this letter to Mr. Taylor:

Figure 4

April 7, 19___

Dear Mr. Taylor:

Paul Simpson showed me your letter of April 5 regarding recent models of portable electric 110V generators and special discount prices for quantity buys.

The new model you mention has not been made, to the best of my knowledge. However, this gives me an ideal opportunity to tell you about a really exciting new product—the Archer 1200 Watt, 12 Volt portable generator. The Archer Unit is an entirely new concept in portable electric equipment and was introduced at the Manufacturer's Exposition in Chicago in February.

It can be used in any truck, camper, or motor home at any time. Easily attached to the alternator with a screwdriver and a pair of pliers, it will operate small jig saws, electric wrenches, drills, sanders, polishers, toasters, coffee percolators, fry pans, trouble lights, and numerous other small electrical power tools and appliances. Any handyman or recreational vehicle owner would be proud to own one and it carries a one year unconditional warranty.

We sincerely believe the need is unquestionable and we are offering a special promotion to introduce the Archer Unit in this area. The suggested retail price is $29.95 and the regular dealer discount is 50-10-5. In quantity buys of 25 or more, it would be 50-10-20 .

As a special introductory offer, however, the price to all our regular dealers until April 30 is a straight 62%. In quantities of 25 or more, we can offer 65%. This offer, of course, will not be repeated.

To answer your original question, our 110V generators are as shown in our catalog. As with the Archer Unit, quantity buys of 25 or more will entitle you to a 50-10-20 discount. Quantity buys, however, require 10 to 14 day lead time.

With the current boom in recreation vehicles and the need for convenient portable equipment, we feel sure you can visualize the huge demand for the Archer Unit in the very near future. Call me or Paul for more details.

Sincerely,

Alan Hart

Paragraph	Sentence	Comment
1	–	A good, smooth way to get into the subject.
2	1	A brief, temporary answer to writer's question. Don't overlook it, but don't give him the whole story or he will not read on any further.
2	2	The "hook"–introducing the new product.
2	2	Broad explanation of product and its origin.
2	3	Specific use and application of product, its benefits, and other selling points.
4	All	Making the offer and giving details.
5	–	The "hurry up" and special terms of the offer.
6	–	Don't ignore writer's original question. Go back and give him all the facts he needs to know.
7	–	Reassure the reader of the security of the future potential for the product. Make the close simple.

Letter writers should take a tip from fiction writers, who seldom *tell* us a character is generous or mean, intelligent or dumb, brave or cowardly—they *show* us—*then* we believe. In short, they give us the *evidence.* A salesman may shout from the rooftops he can give us savings, high quality, or satisfaction, but a customer will not buy or stay sold until the salesman *proves* it. And you will never win your point until you determine and demonstrate a convincing mode of strategy.

A good piece of advice that shouldn't be overlooked: Try to answer your mail *promptly.* Don't let it stack up. If you do, you give the writer (the reader of your reply) cause to worry and conjure up other problems which you don't need.

Before leaving this subject, there are certain other points you should be aware of that are equally as important. They are not a part of the technique itself, but they are basic to any strategy you may employ.

HOW TO STRENGTHEN YOUR WRITING ABILITY

The best way to reinforce or strengthen your writing ability is to improve your reading habits. Like the lumberjack sharpening his axe, reading good literature, current best sellers as well as modern publications in your chosen field, sharpens your writing tools. It improves your vocabulary and your writing finesse, keeps you up to date with changes in the state of the art, and gives you a well rounded background.

Your approach to everyday problems and your ability to evaluate and resolve questions which come before you will be much easier if you come to the task better prepared. Reading other good writers on subjects of the day in addition to your technical specialty will do wonders for your writing ability.

A few years ago Johnson O'Connor, founder of the Human Engineering Laboratories, tested some 100 vice presidents of Eastman Kodak, General Motors, and other large corporations, and found they showed a wider knowedge of words than any other group, including college professors, lawyers and doctors. He examined thousands of others and found high achievers in almost any field score high in vocabulary.

Many other studies have shown college students' performance correlates closely with their vocabulary scores. Aptitudes clearly point out the moral: vocabulary determines how well you succeed in whatever line of work you may be in. Why? A good vocabulary enables us to express ourselves with greater sublety and precision than a limited one. There are some situations you cannot handle at all well if you don't have all the equipment.

Vocabulary is an inner resource, like courage, honesty, faith, integrity, always there when you need it. The more words you know, the more ideas you have, and the more facility you have to think clearly and, having this ability, the easier it becomes to write clearly.

If you want to improve your vocabulary, there are at least a half dozen ways you can do it:

1. Master the facts and words you need to know.

2. Pay close attention to well-informed persons.

3. Use exact and expressive words, rather than vague words.

4. Read with alert attention and, when you run into key words which are unfamiliar, go to a good dictionary.

5. Observe with keen awareness the ways of words in actual use.

6. Studying word formation—in dictionaries and elsewhere—will give you a better understanding of derivative words.

Building a better vocabulary is covered in more detail in Chapter 11. Having a good vocabulary, however, will not insure your writing success. Probably the biggest stumbling block to writing effectively is your own mental attitude. Self-centeredness is the curse of good writing. Most writers write to *impress*, not *express*, and this leads to their own downfall.

How, then, do we recognize the signs that we may be writing for ourselves rather than our reader? Here are some indicators:

• "I, me, or we-itis"—too much of the first person in our letters and reports.

• Talking down to the reader from our "lofty" position.

• Pompous, wordy openings.

• Use of jargon or stuffy language in an effort to sound businesslike.

• Lack of tact and patience.

• Failure to appreciate the reader's point of view or to consider how the reader will react.

A good writer must be as honest as he expects others to be. He must also act on the courage of his own convictions. To be a good writer, however, he has to develop what has come to be known as the "You" attitude.

One famous author described the "you" attitude as the ability to think like the other guy while standing in his shoes. This is a good definition, but to *practice* the "you" attitude, you should:

- have a sincere desire to help the reader.
- learn to be analytical.
- be courteous and tactful.
- use common sense and good judgment.
- develop your imagination and creative ability.

Direct advice on specifics is omitted in this discussion because no craftsman can tell you how to make use of them in a given set of circumstances; for instance, that the information in your letters should be correct and complete, or that you should use basic rules of grammar. Most writers will do these things.

This does not mean we must be purists to write good, plain letters. We can misarrange our syntax without offending our reader or detracting from our dignity. It does mean, however, the quality of our grammar must be such that it is usually acceptable in polite company. No one could ask for anything more.

3

How to Make Certain Your Letters Get Read

Now that you have decided on your strategy, you must consider the next step. Your strategy will be as useless as two tickets to last year's Super Bowl if your letter is not read. Everything else necessarily follows. Therefore, the Second Dimension is: *getting your letter read*. The principal guarantor for this taking place is Brevity. Robert Southey, English poet laureate, perhaps expressed it best when he said:

"If you would be pungent, be brief; for it is with words as with sunbeams–the more they are condensed, the deeper they burn."

In all our dealings with the public, whether it is in oral or written form, a common failing of most of us is to "beat around the bush" or get "lost in the trees." The principal cause of this is because we are not always sure what we want to say. We keep on writing, hoping we will soon find the proper words and, at the same time, hoping our reader doesn't notice our ramblings.

IS YOUR LETTER TOO LONG?

There are only two tests to tell whether a letter is too long: (1) whether it says more than need be said, or (2) it takes too many words for what it has to say.

One of the most effective, yet simple, techniques to employ in planning a letter or memo is to jot down on a pad the following:

1. Letter, memo, or telephone call or reason for writing.
2. Questions to be answered, implied as well as specific.
3. Replies to these questions.
4. Short, but adequate and plausible reasons for the replies.
5. Other information which, although perhaps not directly related to the subject matter, is important enough to warrant comment. This point should receive critical analysis so that it does not let in all the extraneous trivia you are trying to avoid.

Armed with this outline, you are now in good position to formulate a well-organized, brief, and clear letter or memorandum. The major pitfall you want to be wary of is the tendency to introduce and discuss matters, which, although factual, do not materially contribute to the main issue or objectives of the letter.

Figure 1 is an example of an Interoffice Memorandum written by a man in a hurry or in a rage. Either way, he was anything but brief. Read it over and see how you would have written is so as to be brief and clear, but yet get your point across. Figure 2 is one example of how it could have been written (shown at end of chapter).

From a review of Figure 1, it can be seen that Mr. Calls told Mr. Dewitt a lot of information, although perhaps interesting, he really did not need to know, such as:

- restating what Mr. Calls previously said.
- the conditions which the breakdown of equipment caused and the resulting loss of efficiency. In fact, he even prefaced his statement with the remark: "I needn't point out. . ." So why waste both people's time with an official statement?

Mr. Dewitt only needs to know:

1. Previous conversations or communications (October 15 memo).
2. Brief subject reference to bring the matter into proper focus (repair of the air conditioning system in Bldg. 105).
3. What has or has not been done to cause the follow up (system outlet has not been repaired).
4. Specific action expected (take care of repair as soon as possible).

Figure 1

Interoffice Memorandum

To: Mr. U. Dewitt, Administrative Services Department
From: Mr. Vernon Calls, Chief, Purchasing Department

1. Reference is made to our memorandum of October 15, in which we outlined in detail the problems which we were having with our air conditioning and asked that immediate action be taken to get it fixed.

2. I needn't point out this is the summer season and many people are adversely affected by temperature extremes as well as changes. One or two of my clerks have been confined to their homes with colds which were a direct result of the faulty air conditioning. Needless to say, our productivity as well as our efficiency has dropped far more than the cost of repair to the air conditioning system.

3. Again, I request that effective action be taken to remedy this situation at the earliest possible date.

Figure 3 is an example of a letter wherein many words were written down unnecessarily in order to answer a routine inquiry. Fifteen lines were used whereas the subject could have been covered in about one-third the space and still not left out anything important.

Before looking at Figure 4 (which is one way to do it in far less time and verbiage), try rewriting Figure 3 to see how you would have done it.

Figure 3

November 30, 19___

Aviation Supply Office
Attn: Mr. R.E. Winters
Philadelphia, Pa. 19100

Dear Mr. Winters:

Reference is made to your letter, dated November 10, 19___, subject, "Request for Field Pricing Report," in which you requested updated field pricing reports on Letter Contracts 77C8045, -8118 and -8124.

We wish to advise that, since our last communication, we have encountered several difficulties in consummating our audit. One of our field workers was called into jury duty unexpectedly and his replacement, Mr. James, was stricken with appendicitis and had to have an emergency operation. In addition, some of the data which we were given was not taken from the proper input records and had to be reassembled. This was not discovered until last week and Mr. Olds, our supervisor was not aware of it until he examined the report. However, we feel that we have ironed out these problems and that, with no further setbacks, we should be able to furnish the reports by the end of next month.

We sincerely hope this has not caused undue delays or created problems which will prove costly.

Sincerely,

W.A. Hammonds
Vice-Pres., Marketing

Comments on Figure 3:

- Paragraph 1 is too verbose. Nothing is accomplished by stating the subject of the incoming letter and then restating what it was about.

- Paragraph 2 goes into detail as to the reasons for not meeting the deadline for submitting the report. These reasons do not help either party insofar as answering the question is concerned. They would not add to, reduce, or cause any damages to be assessed or result in any loss of business.

- Although paragraph 3 is thoughful and certainly acceptable, the statement is not really necessary.

The things Mr. Winters needs to know:

1. What the letter is about (the date of the letter being answered, a brief subject reference and, in this case, the contract numbers involved because they are important).

2. Reasons for lateness of the report. For the purposes of this inquiry, the reader only needs to know that they were unavoidable.

3. When a complete report will be furnished. It was well to mention that the writer was going to try to send the reports sooner if he could. This shows his intent was well-meaning.

Some of you might well say these two examples were relatively simple and that most communications are not simple enough to brief down that well. Many times this is true. All letters cannot and should not be as brief as Figures 2 and 4. However, it is also true there are many occasions when even a more involved letter can be briefed down to less than 10 or 11 lines and not lose its impact.

Complicated letters, above all, need to be briefed down as much as feasible to help the reader better understand the message the writer is trying to convey. Verbosity is never a remedy for a complicated letter.

Figure 4

November 30, 19___
Aviation Supply Office
Attn: Mr. R.E. Winters
Philadelphia, Pa. 19100
Dear Mr. Winters:

We refer to your letter of November 10, requesting updated field pricing reports on Letter Contracts #77C-8045, -8118 and -8124. For reasons over which we have little or no control, a full, unqualified report will require until the end of December to accomplish. We will certainly try to better that date if at all possible.

Sincerely,

W.A. Hammond
Vice-Pres., Marketing

Figures 5 and 6 are examples of a letter to a supplier concerning his billing procedures that required about 22 lines as originally written. It provided full details and, to some, it might seem more acceptable in that form. However, Figure 6 shows how it could have been written in about half the space of the original and still cover all essential points.

Figure 5

Mr. Ron Hurst
Oilwell Products Co.
P.O. Box 5800
Los Angeles, Calif. 90055

Dear Mr. Hurst:

Attached hereto are your Invoices #6803 and #6812, and related shipping documents, which are returned for correction in accordance with the following.

We have reviewed the contract file and find that it calls for delivery of 50 each #3305-466A Bearing Joints at $6.50 each, 75 each #3305-488A Bearing Joints at $7.75 each, and 100 each #3305-488B Bearing Pins at $4.85 each. The shipping documents however, reflect that Shipment No. 1 showed delivery of 25 each Bearing Joints @ $6.50 each, 30 each Bearing Joints @ $7.75 each, and 45 each Bearing Pins @ (no price shown).

We have discussed this with our Legal people and they insist that the Part Number and the proper price must be shown on both the shipper as well as the invoice, in order for our receiving and accounting departments to be relieved of all accountability. If you over or undershipped prior to the end of the contract, it would be very difficult indeed to establish exactly how many of each unit were shipped and paid for. Neither party would feel he was receiving equitable treatment in the final delivery and settlement of the contract. I'm sure you can understand this, Mr. Hurst.

We trust this has not caused you too much additional cost or inconvenience. However, upon receipt of your corrected invoices, revised to show all the necessary information as outlined above, we will be glad to pay the invoices.

Sincerely,

Howard Hall
Controller

Try rewriting Figure 5 as an exercise to develop your "briefing pen" before peeking at Figure 6.

Mr. Hurst really only needs to know:

1. Identification of the documents being returned.

2. Reason for their return. In this instance, the statement "Invoices should be corrected to correspond . . ." means the description of the items on the invoice should match the description of the items on the shipping documents. By comparison, the reader can readily see what is missing and what needs to be done to comply with the instruction. What you will do when the reader does what he is supposed to do.

Figure 6

May 20, 19___
Oilwell Products Co.

Los Angeles, CA 90055
Attention: Mr. Ron Hurst

Dear Mr. Hurst:

We are returning for correction your Invoices #6803 and #6812 and related shipping documents.

A review of the contract file and coordination with our Legal Department indicates you will be entitled to payment for only those components which are properly identified and indicated as shipped on the attached shipping documents. Your invoices should therefore be corrected to correspond with the shippers, including prices.

We regret this inconvenience but, upon receipt of your invoices, revised to agree with appropriate shipping documents, we will be glad to expedite payment.

Sincerely,

Howard H. Hall

Controller

Encls

DESIGNING "BRIDGES" FOR MORE EFFECTIVE OPENINGS

One of the biggest problems confronting the average letter writer is the tendency to repeat what has already been said, or to make a smooth transition in the opening of a letter. We all need to keep this in mind when we are composing correspondence. After a while, it becomes a habit and we find we can do it more or less automatically.

Try to concentrate on breaking the habit of repeating what is said in a letter you answer. The only reference you need to previous correspondence is for the sake of coupling up and introducing the subject.

For example:

"Your August 3rd letter about cancelled policies brings up an interesting point of law."

"I have referred your recent inquiry about Mr. Glenn Foster to our Personnel Department. Mr. Shaw will look into the matter and call you."

"The Mr. Barker you mentioned in your June 8 letter no longer represents our company."

Cut out words or phrases that add nothing to the reader's understanding or to the sentence structure. Leave out so-called "beside-the-point" information. It may be interesting in a conversation, or in a social letter, but is it really important to the objective of a business letter?

For example:

> On June 25, you were advised that you have furnished 15 each Valve Guides, Part No. 17569 instead of Part No. 17566. You have failed to reply and you are holding up completion of an important prime contract we have with the Army. Your failure to ship the correct parts on time prevents us from meeting our commitment and could endanger our position with the Federal Government.

Comment: The part which follows "You have failed to reply" is so-called beside-the-point information. While it may be true, it does not mean anything to the reader. All the writer need tell the reader is that he (the reader) is not living up to the terms of his *contract* and legal remedies can be sought (implied).

WATCH OUT FOR "ROUNDABOUT" PHRASES

Be especially careful of "roundabout" prepositional phrases, as well as nouns and adjectives that derive from verbs, such as: has knowledge of, affirmation, observation, etc. Use the VERB form know, affirm, see. It is much more effective for the writer, not to mention being more meaningful and interesting to the reader. The reader "feels" the message more quickly and is therefore motivated to act. These "roundabout" prepositional phrases are so easy to recognize and replace with single words that there is little excuse for habitually using them. Here are some examples:

Instead of	*Why not use*
With regard to	about, on
In connection with	of, on
In the event of	if
In order to	to
On behalf of	for
In accordance with	with, by
For the purpose of	for
In the majority of instances	usually

Don't qualify your statements with "if" unless you feel you have to. This confuses the reader unneccessarily and makes it harder for him to agree or disagree with you. For example, here is a letter that really discouraged a friend of mine.

Relative your inquiry pertaining to submission of an article on value engineering for our publication, "Trade Market News," we will be glad to review your article and consider it for publication providing our review committee feels the article has merit and our publication has space at the time for unsolicited material.

Another point, however: if a similar article has been submitted in the past six months we would table consideration of your article. Also, if anything too controversial is contained in the article, or it is too lengthy for our requirements, we would have to return it for revision.

My friend's comment to me was, "I'm glad I didn't ask a complicated question!"

You can use punctuation at times to save words, if it is judiciously done. For example, using a colon for the words "in the following order," or a semi-colon instead of "in order to."

Be on the lookout for those six tiny leprechauns—six meaningless little verbs that aid many letterwriters more than any others in choosing the noun and adjective forms of words. They are *make, take, give, hold, have,* and *be.* Watch them steal the place of the basic verbs in these examples:

Form used	*Better form*
We held the meeting . . .	We met . . .
Rapid growth had a tendency to influence construction . . .	Rapid growth tended to influence construction . . .
The results give one the impression . . .	The results seem to . . .
Their attorney made the reply . . .	Their attorney replied . . .
Mr. Smith will take action to . . .	Mr. Smith will . . .
He is negligent in the details of his work . . .	He neglects details . . .

Some of you might still feel that a truly brief memorandum or letter can only be used if it is either a letter of transmittal or in reply to a routine request for information. On the contrary, there are many occasions where a brief letter (less than 10 lines) is most appropriate. In fact, there are at least 20 different situations where it will be so, albeit mostly in the area of good will. In addition to the normal letter of inquiry, there are:

1. Ordering products or supplies, with or without an order form.
2. Introductions and recommendations of friends or relatives.
3. Invitations to attend meetings, parties or special occasions.
4. Acceptance or declinations of offers of positions.
5. Answering requests for charity.
6. Customer's daughter or son gets married.
7. Customer has been promoted or transferred.
8. Customer is written up in a news article.
9. Customer receives an honor or is elected to some office.
10. People in the neighborhood buy a home.
11. When a product or service pleases you and you want to let your supplier know of your reaction.
12. Birthdays, anniversaries, arrivals of new babies and you want to send your congratulations.
13. Welcome to new residents. Excellent new prospects.
14. Serviceman comes home.
15. Thank you letters to old and new customers.
16. Following up a salesman's call.
17. To make apointments.
18. Someone has done you a favor and you want to show your . appreciation.
19. Customer is ill and you want to show your concern.
20. Customer has had a death in the family.

One word of caution should be offered. Although brevity is frequently appropriate, sometimes necessary, and always a commendable virtue, it should not be practiced at the expense of other requisites of effective writing which will be covered later in more detail.

Figure 2

November 7, 19— —

Interoffice Memorandum

To: Mr. U. Dewitt, Administrative Services Department
From: Mr. Vernon Calls, Chief, Purchasing Department

1. Refer to my October 15 Memorandum relative to repair of the Bldg. 105 air conditioning system.

2. The system outlet has not yet been repaired. The excessive heat is causing absenteeism in my Department. Urgently request this matter be taken care of as soon as possible.

4

Getting Your Message Across in Writing

Even though you may have a good plan and have made the letter "short and sweet," it will avail you little if you fail to *get your message across* to your reader. If what you say is couched in long, unfamiliar, or technical terms, your reader may not understand you. If he is going to react as you want him to, your language must be in simple terms. Therefore, the Third Dimension is: Get Your Message Across, or Keep it Simple!

We don't want to be guilty of briefing a letter down to the point where it becomes confusing. In other words, brevity simply for the sake of brevity is not to be sought. Oftentimes, by leaving out certain words or phrases, we make our meaning indefinite and obscure and, therefore, more complex.

The first key to opening the Simplicity door is to *know your subject* so well you can discuss it, orally or in writing, naturally and confidently. In doing this, however, be sure to keep your language in the vernacular of the reader.

The point here is that you not only need to know the subject well for technical reasons, buy also well enough to *convert* that language into simple, nontechnical terms without *losing* the meaning and intent of the message itself. The technician who can't reduce his language to understandable English is no better off than the English professor who can't understand or explain the ideas or efforts of the engineer. For example, an engineer was trying to explain to an interested prospect part of the induction hardening process:

> The minimum frequency for induction hardening depends on stock diameter. Dividing 180 by the radius of the bar or cylinder in inches will give you the practical minimum frequency in cycle per second. This applies to surface layers heated by induction, but does not take into account the flow of heat by conduction to layers beneath.

Aside from the fact that the explanation may not have been required in the first place, the above explanation could have been simplified by using a formula, e.g.:

> The minimum frequency for induction hardening depends on stock diameter. To clarify it for you, we could express it in equation form:

$$F = \frac{180}{r}$$

> F stands for practical minimum frequency in cycles per second
> r stands for radius of bar inches
> This equation will give you the minimum frequency for surface layers heated by induction, but does not take into account the flow of heat by conduction to the layers beneath.

The fact is that a good, plain letter is no more colloquial than it is formal. It is plain because common speech is its language ingredient. Plain speech, however, should be pleasing to the ear as well as grammatically and factually correct.

The average person's talk is not up to all of these standards, nor is his understanding. A good, plain letter takes a lot more planning and restraint than everyday talk. Our everyday talk is full of little words. Why change them to *big* ones when we write (except when we have to)?

PITFALLS THE AVERAGE WRITER SHOULD AVOID

In most instances, you should write as you talk, eliminating of course the little unnecessary words, such as "well," "and," "so," "er," etc. You should also be wary of certain other pitfalls which the average writer encounters, such as:

1. Using uneccessarily long and complicated sentences. This has got to be the most annoying thing a reader has to face! The longer a sentence, the harder a reader has to work to understand it. Excessive

simplicity, obviously, can be foolhardy, but it's hard to write that simply. A person talks in long, breathtaking sentences but understanding comes about through voice inflection. Writers frequently forget their readers are not guided by this voice inflection. For example:

"Mr. Singer, Vice President, told Mr. Shaw, since there has been some misunderstandings lately, that he would handle all personnel assignments in the future."

Does "he" refer to Mr. Singer or Mr. Shaw? In oral conversation, where Mr. Singer's secretary told the office manager about the decision, she emphasized *He* so there was no doubt that Mr. Singer meant himself.

2.Using long, formal, or unusual words. For example: *more effective* instead of *better, requisition* instead of *requests, anent* instead of *about,* etc.

3. Using "dead-head" words. The term *dead-head,* as you may know, is used in railroading to apply to a passenger occupying a seat without paying a fare. He takes up space and gives nothing in return. A "dead-head" word likewise takes up space and gives nothing in return. For example:

"In the case of the habitual offender, *there is nothing to do* but remove him from the company. *Needless to say,* he is *what might be termed* ineffective as an employee." (The "dead-head" words are *italicized).*

Correction: "Remove the habitual offender from the company. He is not an effective employee (or "He is ineffective")."

4. Using "blunderbuss"terms. A blunderbuss, of course, is an old-fashioned musket that scatters shot because the muzzle flares out sharply. "Blunderbuss" terms scatter their meanings over a wide area. They are vague and ambiguous. They make the reader interpret one meaning from many possible meanings. Quite often the reader is unable to decide what idea or meaning is intended. For example:

"The policy of the Army with respect to the use of oleomargarine is that it should be used in a ratio to butter in a *proportionate amount* to be *predicated* on its *acceptability* to the soldier."

A reader can figure out what is meant by this sentence if he thinks a bit. The trouble is the "blunderbuss" words don't focus on the subject matter properly. It is easier to understand if it is rewritten to:

"The army wants as much oleomargarine to be substituted for butter as the soldiers will accept."

5. Using "smothered" verbs. Smothered verbs are action verbs which are buried inside another word. Smothered verbs lose their

action by becoming noun forms. By definition, a verb specifies what action takes place. It can also indicate a state, a feeling, or simple existence. To meet this definition, a verb must be a relation-showing word. Relation-showing means that when a verb is properly used the action or state denoted is related to persons or things (who or what). For example:

"It has been pointed out that careful, initial *selection* and *classification* are important *procedures* in *eliminating* potential maladjusted personnel in the company."

Apply the questions given above for testing smothered verbs. The relation-showing quality of each smothered verb in the example is poor. Who *selects* what? Who *classifies* what? Who *proceeds?* What *proceeds?* Who *eliminates* what? It can be rewritten to say:

"As has been said, if the organization selects and classifies personnel carefully at the outset, it will have fewer maladjusted people."

6. Using indirect phrasing. Express your idea directly instead of indirectly. Frequent use of *there is* and *there are* weakens emphasis. For example:

"There are four types of tables of organization with which everyone should be familiar." Rewritten: "You (or everyone) should know the four types of tables of organization."

Frequent use of *it is* also indicates an indirect approach. The direct approach is clearer and more forceful. Instead of saying, for example, "It is believed that . . ." or "It is assumed that . . ."; say "The writer believes that (or assumes that) . . ."

7. Using jargon. Jargon (other than technical jargon) is tired, overworked, wasteful language. It doesn't communicate as well as simple language. Frequently, complex words or phrases are used when simple words or phrases would do a better job; complex ones obscure the meaning. They add to the time and effort required in reading. Examples of jargon are:

Jargon	*Should Use*
Along the lines of	Like
In order to	To
In accordance with	By
In the case of	For
With reference to	About
With the result that	So that

Afford an opportunity	Allow
In a manner similar to	Like
In a situation in which	When

WATCH YOUR "FOG COUNT"

These are simple words of advice. The "Fog Count" method is a very handy tool to use to evaluate your writing for its readability. There have been several formulas published in the past 30 years to measure the reading level of writing. I personally prefer the one I developed after I had used them and found them to be somewhat cumbersome or tedious. I only mention this approach because I find it easy to use and it helps to keep me from getting too wordy or complicated.

"Reading," someone once said, "means easy or interesting to read." Perhaps he should have said, "*Easy* reading means easy or interesting to read." In any event, easy reading is *not* easy to write. I recommend you periodically take samples of your work and apply one formula (not necessarily mine) to test it and see how "foggy" it is getting. Armed with this knowledge, then, you can analyze your own writing effort, determine your score, and take steps to improve it.

I have called my method the Parr Easy Appraisal of Readability Level (I jokingly refer to it as the PEARL system, mainly because of my fondness for acronyms). The system is based primarily on two factors: (1) the average number of syllables in each word, and (2) the average number of words in each sentence. The two averages are multiplied by an equalizing factor and the results added together to arrive at a readability level score.

The ideal score, or a reasonable standard score, is 100. The more difficult or complex the writing becomes, the higher the score; conversely, the easier the writing becomes the lower the score. A very easy reading score would be about 70 or less, whereas a difficult reading score would be 107 or higher.

Samples should be taken at reasonable places and in reasonable amounts, e.g., 3 or 4 samples from an article or long letter, 20-25 samples from a book taken in true random fashion. Never take the first or last paragraph (unless it is a short article). Take samples in 100-word groups or, if less than 2 pages or 300 words, count each word and syllable.

To count words, count every group of letters and numbers between typewriter spaces, with the possible exception of proper names, e.g., "John Cameron Swayze" would be counted as one word. To count syllables, count every sound in *all* the words the way you pronounce the word, e.g., capitalization = 6, Connecticut = 4, etc. To count sentences, count each segment of thought that occurs between punctuation marks (except commas and the colons used in quotations).

Computing the readability level score is accomplished in 4 steps:

1. *Average syllables per word.* Divide number of syllables by number of words, and carry to two places, e.g., 260 syllables ÷ 18 words equals 1.44 average SPW.

2. *Average words per sentence.* Divide number of words by number of sentences, and carry to one place, e.g., 172 words ÷ 8 sentences equals 21.5 average WPS.

3. *Multiply each one.* Multiply (1) average syllables per word by 35.0, and (2) average words per sentence by 2.5.

4. *Add* results of step (3). The answer is your readability level score. *Example:* The first paragraph of this subhead under "Watch Your Fog Count" has a readability level score of 94.2.

Computation

No. syllables	126	No. words	87
No. words	87	No. sentences	5
Average SPW	1.45	Average WPS	17.4
Result: (x 35.0)	50.75	(x 2.5)	43.5 = 94.2

IMPORTANT TIPS ON THE USE OF WORDS

Perhaps the best bit of advice to improve your writing style and effectiveness is to *improve your vocabulary.* You can't take time out every day and measure your writing, although it is wise to test it every once in a while. The only practical way to lick the problem is to sharpen up your basic equipment and use it more judiciously when writing letters and reports.

We also don't mean to imply that you should try out new or strange words in your letters but, rather to be able to put more effective meaning in the words you use. It not only helps you in everyday life, but it will add spice, variety, and more complete understanding in your writing.

You might consider it part of your personal improvement program. As stated in Chapter 2, you will also find that letters become progressively easier to write by having more appropriate words or expressions at your disposal.

There are many resons why you need to use plain words, most of them valid, but the most important ones are:

a. They make easy reading and therefore make the reader more comfortable.

b. They "let the light through" and make your message more understandable and acceptable.

c. Plain words, if accurate and expressive, are always in good taste. They don't offend the reader.

d. If you do use unfamiliar words, you will probably lose the reader's attention and interest. Worst of all, it could make you look ridiculous.

Practical experience shows 20 or 21 words to be a fair goal to set for the average sentence. This, of course, is not a hard and fast rule. All sentences in a paragraph should relate to a single idea, but that does not mean all sentences related to that idea must be kept in one paragraph. For easy reading, try to keep your paragraphs to less than 8 lines.

To see a good, or perhaps I should say horrible example of what big words and long sentences can do to a fairly simple letter, read Figure 1. This letter, with certain name changes, was taken from an actual file.

Take note of the "dead-head" words, blunderbuss terms, smothered verbs, jargon, confused meanings, trite phraseology, indirect phrasing. It must have taken two or three times as long to write as a simple, direct approach would have. It certainly will take two or three times as long to read and understand as it should.

While it may not be the best possible version, Figure 2 is an example of how the same letter could have been written in far less time and with far better readability and comprehension on the part of the reader. For your own edification, compare the two and take specific notice of the improvements made.

Figure 1

December 15, 19___

American Industries, Inc.
1500 Ridgeway

Attention: Mr. Sam Brownell
Chicago, Illinois 60606

Dear Mr. Brownell:

Reference your recent correspondence which in essence interimly denied destination acceptance, made allegation of incomplete delivery of the contract end items and/or components, and threatened issuance of a termination notice.

Pertinent contract document #C5432, Section I-1 cites inspection at source and Section I-2 cites acceptance at destination. As our contract file includes a properly issued and distributed final shipping document (XOOSOO1Z), dated October 22, denoting inspection completion by the cognizant quality assurance inspector, I sincerely believe that issuance of a termination notice at this time would be premature and serve no useful purpose. In lieu, I suggest your complaint be reviewed by the inspector in much the same manner as an Unsatisfactory Material Report (UMR).

In addition, I have received information from our Production Department which summarizes the findings from their investigation into your complaint. This material has been reviewed by both the inspector and myself; and we jointly feel that their findings may adequately suffice to clear the contention of alleged delinquency. Since we are willing to pursue this deficiency through to fruition after receipt of data from Mr. Hamilton, I recommend this course of corrective action be adopted, and that Mr. Hamilton's correspondence be routed to this office.

In the interim, a copy of our initial report of findings and clarifications, as above mentioned, is forwarded herewith for your edification and appropriate action.

Please advise as to the action taken or a suspense date as to when we can expect same.

Sincerely,

John F. Bolder

Encl

Figure 2

December 15, 19___

American Industries, Inc.
Chicago, Illinois

Attention: Mr. Sam Brownell

Dear Mr. Brownell:

We refer to your December 10 letter making certain allegations re our contract #C5432 and threatening issuance of a termination notice.

I would like to point out Section I-2 of the contract, which provides for acceptance at destination. Also, to our final Shipping Document No. XOSOOO1Z, showing completion and sign off by your inspector. These factors are inconsistent with the nature of your complaint.

In addition, our Production Department has prepared a report of their investigation into the complaint. I am forwarding it to you for your review. Their findings show no lack of performance on our part. At time of delivery, we were not aware of the position of your engineer, Mr. Hamilton, that material received would not withstand stress tests.

In view of the above facts, I strongly suggest your complaint be handled as a UMR (Unsatisfactory Material Report) rather than considering a termination notice. I am reasonably certain, upon receipt of necessary data from your Mr. Hamilton, we will be able to complete the contract per specifications, even though a slight delay may be encountered.

Please advise as to your decision in this matter.

Sincerely,

John F. Bolder

Experience gives us some good advice on the use of words:
a. Use relatively few articles, prepositions, and conjunctions. In other words, scrutinize them and take them out, e.g.,

Original version:

Dear Mr. Carson:

Mr. Carson, you had indicated that you would notify the undersigned as to the date of completion of the missing 36 units in question. As of this date, we have received no communication from you on this matter. It is therefore requested that you reply in writing to the undersigned stating your intentions in connection with this delinquency. Please furnish us with the dates of your expected shipments and/or the exact status of the situation.

Revised version:

Dear Mr. Carson:

Regarding deliveries on the Alpha contract, you had promised on December 10 you would advise as to delivery date(s) of the 36 missing units. Since we have not heard from you, we must have a written statement from you by December 20, covering your delivery plans in complete detail.

b. Use pronouns instead of repeating nouns, e.g., he, she, they, you, it, instead of Mr. Smith, Mrs. Jones, the auditors, etc.

c. Learn to "factor" expressions, that is, combine adjectives and adverbs. For example: The *overly verbose* man should be referred to as *wordy;* or the *speedy, accurate* secretary could be called *efficient.*

d. Use contractions and short names (without altering the meaning). For example: In addition to words like "can't," "isn't," and "doesn't," words like "est" (for estimate), "incl" (for including or inclusive), and "thru" (for through) are also acceptable abbreviations in modern communications.

e. Use active verbs and voice rather than passive. Action is the first law of the universe. Isn't it better to say, "Let us know when Mr. Daniels can call" than "Mr. Daniels will appreciate being advised when your schedule is open?"

f. Shorten or eliminate needless words. For example, use "long time" rather than "an unusually lengthy period of time."

g. Use figures, symbols, and abbreviations *when* they are *familiar* to the reader. For example, abbreviations like UCLA and AFL/CIO are acceptable because they are understood.

h. Be compact! Don't separate closely related parts of sentences. Single word modifiers (adjectives and adverbs) cause trouble when they get out of place in a sentence, changing the meaning. For example, what is the true intent in each one of the following sentences?

He *only* came to the office on Monday.

He came *only* to the office on Monday.

He came to the office *only* on Monday.

Only he came to the office on Monday.

The most troublesome modifiers, however, are groups of words known as relative clauses, prepositional phrases, etc. These group-word modifiers should read easily and naturally, e.g., "We sent the application to the address *you gave in your letter of March 15,* but it was returned to our office."

CONTROLLING TROUBLESOME MODIFIERS

There are four principal ways to control troublesome modifiers:

1. Boil them down, shortening the sentence as well as simplifying it. Example:

Wrong: Mr. Jones, *who is attorney for the defendant,* said he will appeal the case.

Right: Mr. Jones, *the defendant's attorney,* said he will appeal the case.

2. Keep the key verb near its subject and object or within easy reading distance. *Example:*

Wrong: Interviews with handicapped persons in the nearby cities *will also be scheduled.*

Right: Interviews will also be scheduled with handicapped persons in the nearby cities.

3. Don't try to say too much in one sentence. *Example:*

Wrong: When the insured recovers, her insurance program is continued for not over one year, provided she is not remarried during this period, in order for her to receive full benefits.

Right: (Make two sentences) In order for the insured to receive full benefits, she will be covered for not over one year after she recovers. If she remarries during this period, however, her coverage under the program will be discontinued.

4. Keep an unmistabable kinship between the modifier and the modified. *Example:*

Wrong: The enclosed booklet explains what the family should do *when the worker dies* to collect insurance.

Right: The enclosed booklet explains what the family should do to collect insurance *when the worker dies.*

Several other simple rules to apply in trying to simplify your letters are worthy of comment.

One of the best overall rules to use is to eliminate unnecessary ideas, words, and phrases. Then express the essential words and phrases in more simple language and better sequence.

Another simple rule to observe is "Take That Out!" This statement refers to the bad habit many of us have of starting every phrase or clause with the all-purpose word "that." The word "that" can be used as an adjective, adverb, conjunction, or a pronoun.

In its conjunctive form, *that* is used as a function word to introduce a subordinate clause expressing purpose, result, or cause. It is this particular use of the word that creates the most problems. Therefore, it is a good idea, when editing a letter or a report, to question whether each use of the word is really necessary or beneficial and, when it is not, to take it out. An example of this is seen in the following:

"If you convince the customer *that* you have considered all sides of his proposal, he will be satisfied *that* you have done everything in your power . . ."

Removal of the two *thats* in the above sentence improves not only the grammatical construction but the sound as well.

A third rule: Don't use adjectives or adverbs any more than necessary. Adjectives are words which qualify nouns and, in their place, perform a useful function; adverbs are words which qualify verbs, adjectives, and other adverbs. Whenever you use an adjective or adverb in your statement, you add a further dimension which has to be interpreted and understood by the reader. You are making his job that much harder.

Rule four: Avoid the use of dangling participles whenever you can, especially in your complimentary close. Bring every letter to a definite, positive, "upbeat" conclusion. Example:

Avoid	*Say*
Looking forward to serving you . . .	It will be a pleasure to serve . . .

Thanking you again . . .	Your letter is appreciated . . .
Hoping to find you . . .	Good luck on your trip (etc) . . .
Regretting our inability to . . .	I hope we will be able to . . .
Awaiting your reply . . .	We await your reply with . . .

TYING THOUGHTS TOGETHER

One parting thought in the area of simplicity. Try to *tie thoughts together* so your reader can follow from one to another without getting confused. There are three practical ways to do this and there is an easy way (or "gimmick" if you like) to remember them—you can "P–E–G" them by:

P–arallel construction,

E–choes, or

G–uideposts.

Parallel construction consists of using a similar voice, tense, and mood to make the information flow more smoothly between the writer and the reader. Example:

"This will enable us *to give you* prompt delivery, *to show you* we are always responsive to your needs, and *to let you* enjoy the benefits sooner than you may have expected."

Echoes are words, usually pronouns, which stand for or reflect back to a word in the last paragraph or sentence. For example, if "Wisconsin Manufacturer's Management Seminar" was used in paragraph one, the single word *seminar* in paragraph two or three would be clear to the reader.

Guideposts cannot stand alone. They usually consist of:

- Exceptions, such as however, nevertheless
- Cause or effect, such as hence, therefore
- Time or place, such as next, later, at, then
- Additions, such as besides, furthermore

Use of any or all of these methods isn't necessary in every letter, of course, but if the opportunity presents itself, use of them will promote clarity and cohesiveness in your letters.

5

Winning Your Reader to Your Point of View

An objective frequently overlooked in modern day communications is: getting the reader on your side, or winning him over to your point of view. The lack of it frequently accounts for things failing to happen. The spark for this conversion from mild interest to active support is a trait that springs from the heart and is called Sincerity.

English minister John Tillotson long ago defined it thus: "Sincerity is to speak as we think, to do as we pretend and profess, to perform what we promise, and really to be what we would seem and appear to be."

If you would like to become a good or better than average letter writer, you should realize that you are not writing to an office or an institution but, no matter where located, to an individual—a living, breathing human being. He is not writing just because he doesn't like you, even though it may seem that way.

Transpose your roles for a moment and look at the problem from his vantage point. Reversing the perspective often sheds a different light on a subject. If you can be patient, understanding, and helpful, you can usually find a satisfactory solution. If you don't want to, or can't be, the problem could grow into something bigger. This, of course, is unnecessary and costly.

The cardinal principle is: *be human.* Use words that stand for human beings, like Mrs. Thomas or Mr. Simon, or the personal pronouns he, she, we, you, etc. Enable the reader to relate to you as an individual, not as a plant, ghost, or commodity. Then speak to that person's problem.

We see an example of this in the case of a Mrs. Duncan, who had purchased a capri set from a local department store. Later, without stopping to check, she put it in her washing machine. When the capris shrank, she was quite annoyed and sent them back to the store, feeling that the store was remiss in not telling her ahead of time that the set was not washable.

The store policy could have been "Let the buyer beware" and, therefore, put the burden of proof on the customer. However, the manager realized the store would not only lose the argument, but also a customer and perhaps the business of her friends as well. Following is a sample of the letter that was sent to her:

Dear Mrs. Duncan:

We acknowledge receipt of the capri set that shrunk when washed in your washing machine. The material is not washable, as some of the others were, but was to be dry cleaned. Our sales staff is instructed to make this clear to every purchaser. Sometimes, however, a salesperson assumes that the customer has been told something because he had just told another customer and didn't repeat it. We're not sure, of course, but this could easily have happened in this instance.

We are sorry, Mrs. Duncan, if you have suffered any disappointment or inconvenience as a result. We will make whatever adjustment you prefer—by sending you a new capri set, same color, which we shall send to you as soon as we receive your instructions, or by crediting your account.

Sincerely,

Alice B. Hale

Let's look closely at this letter. Why did we write it this way?

Paragraph one, first sentence: "Boil" the reasons for the letter down into a simple sentence. Don't dwell on it by making it either too formal or too lengthy. The long drawn out or formal approach creates the image of "arm's length" negotiation and gives the reader the feeling of rejection.

Sentences two and three: Matter of fact statements as to what caused the problem. It would have been easy to adopt a superior or a patronizing tone at this point.

Sentences four and five: These are giving the customer a chance to save face by showing (i) what *should* have been done (and probably *was* done) and (ii) what *could* have happened.

Paragraph two, sentence one: Show *your* concern for the feelings of the reader—in other words, win her over.

Sentence two: Wind it up as quickly as you opened it up. Tell her what to do or what alternatives she has. Keep it as simple as you can. Sincerity always comes through much better in simple language.

IMPORTANCE OF THE "YOU" ATTITUDE

Attitude is of utmost importance. The YOU attitude, for example, is the correspondent's constant awareness of the reader's viewpoint in order to determine and use the most effective ways of getting the reader to think or act as the writer wishes. Until you think in his terms you will never really understand the reader's problem. If you don't understand his problem, how then can you really be sincere?

The use of the pronoun YOU, however, deserves special attention. Careless or thoughtless application of it may have an *adverse* effect on the reader. For example, the statement "You sent only two copies of the brochure, not the four copies you mentioned" could insinuate that the other party is responsible. The general rule of thumb here is: if the idea is used in the positive sense, use of the word YOU will not create the wrong impression; if the idea is used in the negative sense, think carefully before you use it.

In any case, the YOU attitude requires imagination, discrimination, and the profit motive. For example:

Wrong: We offer these articles only in six dozen lots, for to sell them in smaller quantities would eat up our profit.

Right: It is only by selling these articles in nothing smaller than six dozen lots that we can offer them to you at these unusually low prices.

To repeat an old cliche: to err is human—but still true. Admit mistakes. Don't hide behind meaningless words to cover up and confuse the reader. The writer who admits mistakes in plain language is more sure of convincing others of his sincerity. For example: A dealer wrote this letter: "Our office gave you the wrong quote because I thought your request was from *Stan* White, instead of *Sam*

White. Needless to say, when I discovered my error, I wanted to let you know immediately."

Don't you agree that the above dealer is apt to be honest about his final quotation than if he had ignored or tried to cover up the error?

Never overwhelm your reader with intensives and emphatics that you cannot prove, like the "biggest," "greatest," "highest," etc. Likewise, don't gush with insincere flattery, indulge in slang, or trade in trick phrases.

Don't be subservient or arrogant in your words or tone. Strive to express yourself in a friendly yet dignified manner. If you are supposed to be a businessman, act like one.

We see in the following example a condition where a debtor, Jim McElroy, had run into some difficulties and failed to pay up an outstanding bill of several hundred dollars. Mr. Greenwood, the Credit Manager, could have written Mr. McElroy a curt, businesslike letter, or even an unfriendly one. However, through a third source, he discovered that Mrs. McElroy had had a recent major operation and there was good cause for Mr. McElroy's delinquency in paying his bill. He, therefore, altered his course.

Dear Mr. McElroy:

We have just heard from Mr. Elton Jones, who calls on you, of your wife's operation. We were glad to hear the operation was a success and that Mrs. McElroy is now on the road to recovery. We realize this caused you considerable anguish as well as expense. We sincerely regret we were not informed of it before a reminder of your bill was mailed to you.

Let me hasten to assure you—don't let it give you any concern. We know you will attend to this matter as soon as you are in a position to do so.

Please accept my best wishes for Mrs. McElroy's early recovery.

Sincerely,

Arthur T. Greenwood

The most important part of this letter is in the fact that the *reader's* problem was given *first* place. Mr. Greenwood recognized the real cause for the delinquency and acted accordingly.

He also couched the whole letter in positive terms to soothe the customer's obviously upset and nervous condition, to encourage him to plan on a hopeful future, and to retain him as a friend and as a satisfied customer.

Of course, being businesslike and understanding doesn't mean you can't use "talky" words, or common expressions which the reader can readily understand. Replace cliches with fresh phrases. Use personal words where you can appeal to the emotions as well as logic.

A few years ago a term came into current usage, called "Shirt-sleeve English." As you might suspect, it means taking off your coat, rolling up your sleeve, discarding formalities, and getting down to the "nuts and bolts" or, in today's terms, the "nitty gritty." The best part about "Shirt-sleeve English" is that it brings results. Don't be afraid to use it. Letters written in cheerful, constructive, and confidence-restoring tones will often dissolve resistance.

TELLING A CUSTOMER YOU CAN'T

Every businessman knows all customers can't afford credit, and the businessman can't afford the risk, but the question always comes up: How do I tell a customer I *can't* give him credit and yet not offend him and chase him away? About the only answers here are (i) above all, be sincere, and (ii) keep it simple.

Here is an example of how one Credit Manager explanied to a cash customer why he couldn't graduate to a credit customer, but still managed to keep him in the family of good, regular customers:

Dear Mr. Stern:

Mr. Williams, our representative in your area, recently turned in your order for vises, hand tools, and assorted hardware. We sincerely appreciate this order, along with your request for credit.

As part of the customary credit verification, we asked you for a financial statement. On the basis of the information received, we regret to say we must defer granting you a line of credit at this time.

Our decision, Mr. Stern, is based mainly on two factors; the comparatively short time you have been in business in this area, and your present limited capital.

Where we postpone the granting of a credit account, we suggest the customer continue to do business on a cash basis for a short period and we will watch for further developments. We hasten to assure you we welcome your business, either by remittance with order or C.O.D., as a temporary type of arrangement.

It is entirely possible we have overlooked something. If, by chance, there are factors which have escaped us or to which you think we have not given enough weight, please write us. Better still, if it is more convenient, call on us here in person. We will be glad to have any reasonable basis on which to reconsider this matter.

I am sure you can see our position. I will be only too glad to cooperate with you in every way consistent with our credit policy.

Sincerely,

John Thomas, Credit Manager

Let's take a close look at the above letter to see why it was written this way:

Paragraph One: Short, informal opening. Brings subject into focus without an elaborate introduction.

Paragraph Two: Brief explanation of the problem and the action that had to be taken.

Paragraph Three: Highlights the reasons behind the decision. Once again; don't *overemphasize* the negative. Paragraphs 2 and 3 are the "bitter pills." Don't stretch them out unnecessarily.

Paragraph Four: Gives the customer a firm basis for continuing doing business in spite of the roadblock you just threw at him.

Paragraph Five: Gives customer chance to save face, and you a chance to change your mind if you made a mistake.

Paragraph Six: A simple "shake hands" close. Leave the customer with a good taste in his mouth.

Every business letter (except the most routine) must both *tell* and *sell.* The writer must appeal to the reader's wants and needs. Try to visualize your reader as a real person and ask yourself: Who am I talking to and what are his needs? Adapt to the reader's language and, if you know him well enough, his character.

Don't get the idea that every letter needs a finishing touch. The sincerity of your letter should suffice. However, a pleasant ending is important and the use of a conclusion that will motivate a response is always a better way.

BUILDING GOOD WILL

Before we leave this subject, I would like to stress once more something which should, by this time, be pretty obvious. This is the fact that the surest way to build business, maintain it, or regain it, is through the continuing practice of good will or, as I choose to call it, the *human* side of a letter.

A new customer appreciates a warm and friendly letter because he feels he has now been accepted as a member of the family; the regular customer likes it because you are showing you appreciate his business; the "temporarily lost" customer responds because you have gone out of your way to recognize him and the value of his business.

It is always a good idea to write to customers who have not been shopping at your place of business for several months. In addition to making him feel good and perhaps bringing him back into the fold, you might find out something important as to why he hasn't been around.

The following letter is written in what is obviously a delicate situation, requiring tact and diplomacy. No one really knows why Mr. Wilson suddenly stopped doing business, so you must assume that ruffled feelings must be soothed, and a disgruntled customer won back. This kind of letter must be appropriate to the sort of relationship which existed between the customer and the owner or some officer of the store, or you run the risk of offending him even more and that, of course, you want to avoid at all costs.

Dear Mr. Wilson:

I have just heard to my amazement that you feel you haven't been getting the same attention you received when we were a smaller firm. I was wondering why I hadn't seen you lately.

I am truly sorry if anyone in our organization has not been taking care of you the way you deserve to be as a loyal customer for many years. If this is so, I offer my personal apology, and I hope you will give us another chance.

I look forward to seeing you personally the next opportunity you have to drop in on us. I would enjoy discussing our business relationship and I will see to it you are taken care of to your complete satisfaction and, incidentally, mine as well. We have had a very pleasant and profitable relationship for a number of years, and I would feel hurt—more for personal than business reasons—if through some fault of ours, that relationship was endangered in any way.

Hope to see you soon.

Cordially,

A.B. Cummings

In the final analysis, you can only be as sincere and truthful as you intend to be and that desire stems from your mental attitude. If it is as it should be, your letters will automatically reflect that sincerity. Conversely, if you don't feel the desire, you cannot easily make your letters belie the fact.

6

Writing Executive Letters That Make the Reader Respond Favorably

Strangely enough, we can have properly used strategy, brevity, simplicity, and sincerity in our letters and still have weak letters. The Fifth Dimension, or the missing link needed to put it all together in order to grab the reader and make him want to respond is *Strength*.

The magic ingredient that gives a letter the strength it so sorely needs is Satisfaction. This satisfaction, however, takes several forms— two to be exact. One of the most important forms and the one we think of first of all is giving the customer what he wants.

If you convince the reader you have considered all sides of his problem or questions, and have then given him an acceptable solution or alternatives, he will be satisfied. He may not have completely resolved his problem, but at least he will be sure you have done everything you could do.

Convincing the reader you have done these things, however, normally requires a well written letter. It will not be accomplished if you have used weak language or poorly constructed sentences or, worst of all, used an organization of thoughts and words he doesn't readily comprehend or agree with.

This therefore leads us into the second and far more subtle form of satisfaction—*Mental* Satisfaction. A weak letter can be created in many different ways and, unless we are aware of the pitfalls which may exist, we could end up with an ineffective letter.

Weak letter-writing results from using abstract or indefinite words, hedging around the basic problem, going to extremes, using passive verbs or broad statements, using improper grammar or construction, employing long words and phrases, or designing a poor arrangement of thoughts.

Use of any or all of these faulty practices annoys the reader to some degree because:

- he becomes mentally upset.
- he doesn't have specific and definite explanations or directions.
- he isn't sure of your meaning.
- he lacks confidence in you because you haven't won this faith & trust.

NINE STEPS TO GAIN POWER AND STRENGTH

The obvious remedy for the above forms of dissatisfaction is putting *Strength* into your letters. Getting strength in your letters involves many things, but they may be summed up by:

1. Striving for balance, i.e., using long and short words, sprinkling some nontechnical with the technical, etc.
2. Using the proper words wherever possible.
3. Using active rather than passive verbs.
4. Giving clear and definite statements.
5. Employing correct grammar and sentence structure.
6. Answering *all* questions asked.
7. Making it easy for the reader to agree or react favorably.
8. Think positively, write positively. For example:

    Not: Due to the fact that printing charges are quite high, we have no other alternative than to make a slight charge of 50¢ for this manual.

    But: Although printing charges are quite high at the present time, you can still get this excellent manual for only 50¢.

9. Designing a good arrangement or controlling emphasis by:

    - Position. Putting important points near the top, etc.
    - Fullness of treatment. Giving both good and bad points; the high, low, and medium, etc.
    - Appearance. Neat letters have a subtle appeal.
    - Phraseology. Building up to your best point gradually, if you are trying to put across an idea.

- Parallel structure. Effective because of its sound.
- Antithesis. Contrasts often convince more than "A–B–C" statements.
- Questions. Effective because, in most cases, the reader will react.
- Quotations. Most everyone respects the opinion of an authority.
- Illustrative techniques. Better use of:

    Paragraphing
    Itemized lists
    Capital letters
    Underlining
    Punctuation

Getting down to cases, a good example of a weak letter is contained in Figure 1. Is it fair to say this letter doesn't do much to satisfy your interest or curiosity?

Compare this letter with the revised version in Figure 2. More than likely, you will find the latter more satisfying. The difference is not so much in what the two writers have to say as in the way they say it. The weak writer gives you a general idea of conditions on the road, but Mr. Adams gives you an exact picture, etching it out with specific, concrete words.

TELLTALE FOOTPRINTS OF A WEAK WRITER

The weak writer often deals in abstract nouns like *experience, opinion,* and *disease.* Mr. Adams chooses concrete, specific words like *Mr. Simes, smallpox,* and *Anaconda copper range.* Instead of smothering his reader's perception with a phrase such as *seem to be efficiently managed,* he cuts through the fog with the simple, meaningful phrase *well run.* He is not satisfied to say cases of disease are *infrequent.* He specifies the fact there was only *one* case of typhoid fever.

Figure 1

March 12, 19____

Casco Engineering Co.
Helena, Montana

Dear Mr. Wilcox:

It is believed you will be interested to know that the Corps of Engineers Commission which was recently sent up to Montana to look into the Northern Railroad matters has just returned.

A favorable report has been made by the engineer in charge of the Commission, whose background and experience qualifies him to appraise the conditions of the road. He expressed the opinion that the amount expended on the construction project appears to compare favorably with similar undertakings. He further stated that it is his opinion that provisions for the workers and facilities for safeguarding health were better than normally is the case in similar projects.

His report indicates that instances of disease are infrequent, and there is no evidence that intoxicating beverages are allowed in the immediate construction area. The hospitals seem to be efficiently managed, and the compensation plan is apparently satisfactory to the participants.

If you feel you would like a complete copy of the report, let me know and I will send it to you.

Cordially yours,

Joshua J. Jefferson

Figure 2

March 12, 19____

Casco Engineering Co.
Helena, Montana

Dear Mr. Wilcox:

It will interest you to know, Mr. Wilcox, the Commission which I sent up this year to Montana to look into the Northern Railroad matter has just returned.

The engineer on this Commission was Mr. Simes, who was formerly Chief Engineer of the Chicago and Northwestern Railway, and who now is in charge of the appraisal of eastern roads under the Interstate Commerce Commission. He tells me our Montana road could not have been built for less money if handled by a private concern. He has never seen any railroad camps where the men were provided with as good food, and where there was such care taken of their health.

They have had no smallpox and but one case of typhoid fever. No liquor is allowed on a line of the road. The road, in his judgment, has followed the best possible location. Our hospitals are well run. The compensation plan adopted for injuries is satisfactory to the men.

I have directed that all possible speed be made in connecting the Anaconda Copper Range with Butte. This involves the heaviest construction we will have to undertake. By the middle of next year, however, no strikes intervening, this part of the work will be done.
Cordially,

Jackson P. Adams

Abstract nouns specify qualities, conditions, actions, or relation. If they were not useful they would not be a part of our language, but most letterwriters use them when verbs or adjectives would be more forceful. For a simple example, take the word *pride.* It loses none of the shining quality of words in the sentence: *Pride goeth before a fall.* But say *He is a man of pride,* and the shine dims somewhat. The adjective form is better: *He is a proud man.*

Several other points about Figure 2 should be mentioned:

Par.	Sentence	Comment
2	1	Mr. Simes was specifically identified. This helps the reader. The phrase "this Commission . . ." refers back to the same body in the first paragraph. This is an "echo" and avoids repetition. "who is now in charge of . . ." identified Mr. Simes' current job assignment.
2	2	"road could not have been built . . ." and "he has never seen . . ." are strong, unqualified statements.
3	1/3	The words "they" and "The road . . ." are echoes.
4	2	Satisfactory close. Tells what is involved, what can be expected, and when it should be completed.

I am not vain enough to try to tell you that *all* letters can be completely rid of all abstract nouns, or even a great majority of them. Abstract nouns name too many of the subjects with which we deal in everyday business: agreements, eligibility, systems, cooperation, management, etc. You can, of course, think of many more.

Far more damaging to letters and much easier to replace than abstract nouns, are generalities. A letter by its very nature lends itself to specific treatment. It is intended for one person. It often deals with his problem alone. The reader who has waited impatiently for his claim or his problem to be settled is not very easily soothed by such a general statement as:

"This office is making every effort to handle your claim expeditiously."

There is no excuse for telling a man his application "must be filed within 30 days of the date of his letter or within 90 days of the date of his original application, whichever is later" when facts show his deadline date is July 15. Worse than that, you really cloud the issue by telling a man whose claim is denied that "denial of the claim is premised upon the obvious proposition . . ."

If you are writing about 12 men who fail to prove their cases for a dozen different reasons, the phrase "absence of satisfactory evidence," stuffy though it might be, will get by. But if you are writing about one man, or even two or three, by all means by specific.

Admittedly, there are times when, as they say, discretion is the better part of valor. You may not want to risk offending your reader by telling him he has a "crackpot" idea, especially if he is a good customer of yours or a long time business associate. Your own best judgment enters the picture, as well it should. You may be forgiven for saying, for example: "Your expression of opinion will receive consideration when the occasion arises."

If you are ordering something mailed to you, or want something definite done, by all means leave no doubt as to what you want. For example, if you are ordering certain supplies or goods without an order form, the best procedure is to make one of your own, such as in the following example:

Star Route 1
Aurora, IL 60650
November 20, 19___
Branch and Nixon
Adamston, IL 60655

Gentlemen:

Please send me the following items from your Fall and Winter Catalog, C.O.D.:

Catalog No.	*Quan.*	*Item*	*Color*	*Price*
75G2100	1	AM/FM Radio	Black	$29.95
75G212	1	Album Rack	Red/White	14.75
75G2144	1	Clock	Gold	12.75

75G2122	1	Needle	–	12.50
			Total	69.95
			Tax	3.50
			Total	$73.45

Mail these items by December 10, if possible, as they are intended to be Christmas presents. Thank you.

Sincerely,

William P. Benson

WHEN TO USE ACTIVE AND PASSIVE VERBS

Another way to strengthen your letters and, at the same time, shorten your sentences, is to use fewer *passive* verbs and more *active* verbs. The very word passive suggests an indecisive approach. The word active suggests verbs of that form will make a letter stronger.

Taking a page out of history, the following sentence is written in both forms. Is there any question in your mind which is the more effective?

Active: Fourscore and seven years ago, our fathers brought forth on this continent a new nation . . .

Passive: Fourscore and seven years ago, a new nation was brought forth on this continent by our fathers . . .

We may never write immortal sentences like Mr. Lincoln, but we can do a thorough job of spoiling the natural order of simple sentences like these:

Active	*Passive*
Mr. Jones was at the meeting	The meeting was attended by Mr. Jones
In this case, the District Court upheld the lower court's decision that the defendant was negligent.	In this case, the decision of the lower court that the defendant was negligent was upheld by the District Court.

We are not trying to say all passive verbs are to be avoided like the plague. Passive verbs are sometimes useful, such as:

1. When the *doer* or the action is less important than the recipient:

The defendant has three children. The oldest son *is called* John.

(here *the oldest son* is the most important point).

2. When needed emphasis is gained by putting the name of the act or of the doer at the end of the sentence:

Divorce laws *are enacted by* the States (The passive voice here helps the writer emphasize the laws are not Federal).

3. When the doer is not known or may not be named:

Much *has been said* for and against legalized abortion.

It is very easy for anyone to lapse into the passive voice without being aware of it, thereby sapping strength from the sentences which make the doer or the action a "byproduct," or hide the doer behind an impersonal passive: "Your uncle's letter was read *by the Manager* with interest." The manager here has been made a byproduct, yet he is the *doer.* Why not say, "The Manager read your uncle's letter"?

Another pitfall that many people stumble into is explaining the answer before giving it. Give answers straightaway; then explain, if necessary, and then only to the degree that is required. Here is an example of how many letters are prepared in reply to a simple question:

Before: "This is in reference to your application for certain benefits under the Veterans Preference Act. Public Law 82–284 provides that 10 point veterans are entitled to $100. per month while attending an accredited school or university. In accordance with the above, your application has been approved for payment."

After: "Your application for benefits under the Veterans Preference Act has been approved. You will receive your payments beginning on or about September 1, 19___"

Still another loophole many writers work their way into is *hedging.* And hedging is just that–a loophole to escape from statements which are slightly doubtful or not fully inclusive. Hedging sometimes may be legitimate, but many letterwriters hedge their statements from force of habit rather than for any good reason. They seem fond of using the adverbs apparently, normally, generally, and ordinarily.

Hedge statements lose forcefulness. The reader may get the idea the writer doesn't know what he is talking about. For example:

"Apparently, you failed to enclose the money order for $15.00 mentioned in your letter of September 15."

Did the writer of that sentence have some doubt as to whether the reader actually *did* enclose the money order? In such case, he might have turned the statement around into a sure fact:

"We did not receive the money order mentioned in your letter of September 15. Did you perhaps forget to enclose it?"

At worst, needless hedging leads to needless correspondence by raising needless questions in the reader's mind. If a statement or a report is invalid or incomplete, why not say so?

SEVEN RULES ABOUT WRITING LETTERS OF CRITICISM

A few words should be mentioned about letters which involve criticism of some type. They have to be written, of course, but no one likes to get them. Here are some rules to follow in writing them:

1. Never criticize unless there's a good chance it will do some good.
2. Try to praise before you criticize. In other words, "sugarcoat" the pill.
3. Always criticize constructively. Anyone can nag about something, but that doesn't do anybody any good. More to the point, it annoys both parties and creates other problems.
4. Never criticize a man's motives. As far as you know, the only thing that occurred was his execution went bad.
5. Criticize gently, but tactfully. It's usually more effective to point out what happened and ask what can be done about it.
6. Never criticize if you know the reader is upset about something else at the time. He will not understand your motive.
7. Criticize yourself too, if it is not too artificial or contrived to do so and make the reader believe you mean it.

In summarizing the points we have covered in this Chapter, here are some reminders to help strengthen your letterwriting ability:

1. Get some "rhythm in your writing." Mix your long words and sentences with shorter ones. It gives balance and adds class. Too much of one subject gets boring.
2. Use specific, concrete words instead of loose, general, all-inclusive terms. This ties in with hedging.
3. Use more active verbs than passive ones. Encourage action, not apathy.
4. Don't explain your answer before you give it. In other words, don't get the cart before the horse. Give answers right away, then explain.
5. Make sure you have answered all the questions the reader has raised, arranged your letter properly, and made it easy for the reader to agree.
6. Finally, apply the "Five-sided Formula" and review your letters critically. That is, watch your Strategy, Brevity, Simplicity, Sincerity,

and Strength. If practicable, set the letter aside for a few hours or a day and look it over with a clear and objective eye.

For your information and assistance in composing a better letter, I have put together a list of about 200 words which are overworked, used incorrectly, or are longer than need be. You will find it in Chapter 12. I call it my USED WORD LIST. If you can't find a new word from this list or devise one of your own, you may decide to fall back on one of the old cliches, but it won't help your letters very much.

7

Writing Sales Letters
with SNAP

Sales letters are considered a separate category unto themselves for several very good reasons. The most important reason is the fact that they have a completely different objective than the ordinary business letter. They must, to be successful, *motivate* the reader to buy.

The title *Writing Sales Letters With* **Snap** does not mean to imply that they are really *easy* to write, even though to some they might well be. The salient point here is that, above all, they must contain *Snap*, or the four elements beginning with those letters:

S—imple

N—ovel

A—ppealing

P—rovocative

A sales letter has to be *simple* for the irrefutable reason that the message *must get through*. No one has ever sold anything when it was couched in complex terms. Even when complicated programs or ideas are sold, as they all must be, they are presented in simple, cogent, easy-to-understand terms. If you don't believe it, try it sometime and see what results you get.

As mentioned in a previous chapter, the first and foremost action in putting your point across is getting the reader's attention. This is being *novel.* If you do this, then you can be reasonably sure he will read the main part of your letter. This fact is most important in a sales letter because the reader did not ask for nor does he expect to get your letter. You must appeal to the reader's self interest in order to gain and hold his attention.

A sales letter must be *appealing* because you want to *hold* the reader's attention, get him involved and interested, and make him want to buy what you have to offer. What will people buy? People don't buy *Things*—they buy what those things will do for them.

They don't buy *Clothes*—they buy such things as Style, Durability, Impressiveness, or simply Attractiveness.

They don't buy a *Trailer*—they buy Enjoyment, Relaxation.

Customers only buy *Benefits* or *Uses.* The product itself is, in reality, incidental to its function. What it will do for HIM or HER is what makes the buyer want to part with hard, cold cash.

Now that you've aroused the reader's interest and desire by being *simple* and *novel,* and made him want to buy what you're offering by making it *appealing,* how do you induce him to act? That is, how can you be *Provocative?*

One of the best ways is to *ask* for the order. Put some sort of *incentive* or *time limitation* on your offer so that you make the reader feel is is letting something *important* get away from him if he doesn't order at once. In other words, if you give him any reason to procrastinate or NOT do someting, he will. As a famous man once said, "If you're selling something, try to make it so that you would rather be the *Buyer* than the man who sold it."

THREE MAIN CATEGORIES OF SALES LETTERS

All business letters are, in a sense, sales letters. Sales letters, however, are distinguished from other business letters by the fact that their objective is *direct* and more or less *immediate.* Sales letters, for the sake of discussion, may be classified into three broad categories:

1. The most common and largest variety of sales letter is the one used in direct-mail selling.

2. The second largest group, although there is no way to prove it, is the letter written to sell a specific product, idea, or service to an individual or a select group of people.

3. The third category is the letter written to help a salesman make the sale, or to bring back a dormant customer into the active category.

We should look briefly at each category. Let's start with the last one first; mainly because it in not quite as prevalent.

No selling job is ever completely finished. The alert businessman keeps analyzing his accounts. After he finds a likely candidate, he might write a letter, such as that shown in Figure 1.

Let's turn the microscope on this letter for a brief moment. First of all, what is the purpose or motivation for it? Mr. Smith's main objective, quite obviously, is to increase his sales without saying so. The reader could care less at this point. Secondly, he wants to retain Mr. Salmon's good will and future business. Finally, he wants to help put the sales representative, Mr. Andrews, in a closer working relationship with the customer.

The first paragraph opens on a cheerful and positive note and shows Mr. Smith's appreciation for the volume of business contributed by Mr. Salmon. Notice how this approach will gain his attention.

The second paragraph is simple, brief, and yet covers the essential points: (1) thanking the customer for his continuing patronage; (2) offering Mr. Smith's cooperation in an effort to *build up Mr. Salmon's sales;* (3) telling Mr. Salmon what Mr. Smith intends to do; and (4) offering the assistance of the sales representative in doing it.

Figure 1

March 15, 19___

Dear Mr. Salmon:

I am happy to note the steady increase in the frequency and size of your orders since we started doing business together. It is satisfying to me to realize that our product line is being well received by your customers and that you are doing so well with it.

I have two reasons for writing today—one, to thank you for your patronage and two, to offer our cooperation in any way that will build your sales of our products even further. Under separate cover, I am sending you some advertising aids that can be used in window and counter displays; mats for newspaper ads; and suggested spot announcements for your local radio station. Ed Andrews, our representative, will drop in on you next Tuesday to help you set up these displays and to offer his assistance in whatever capacity he may be of help. If there is anything special you may need, don't hesitate to get in touch with me, or let Ed know.

I look forward to the continuance of our pleasant and, I hope, mutually profitable relationship. With all good wishes, I am

Sincerely,

Jack Smith

The closing paragraph is a friendly and cordial sign off, leaving the customer with the proper mental attitude and feeling toward the writer. The letter is short and to the point, but it will go a long way toward fostering a continuing and profitable business association.

The alert businessman never feels smug about his regular customers. He does not leave the initiative to them, being content merely to take orders. He says, "It costs less to keep a customer than to get one."

If he starts a new line, if he makes an improvement in one of his products, or if he has a plan for changing or expanding his service, the alert businessman lets his satisfied customer know about it.

Maintain contact with your customers and, so far as you can, make the contacts personal. Some firms regard regular monthly communication with their customers a minimum requirement for good customer relations. To the routine mail they add interesting enclosures. For signatures they do not use only the firm name, but rather the name of an officer of the firm, the head of a department, or a salesman. Anniversaries and birthdays are usually always remembered.

Department stores keep in touch with their charge customers by sending them advance notices of sales, seasonal announcements, and letters about special services they may be offering.

Customers often vanish without notice. Some of them die and some go bankrupt. Others move away or get into some other business environment, so a certain amount of lost business must be anticipated. But there are other lost customers who must not be given up without prolonged and persistent effort. Figure 2 is a good example of how to maintain good will and show a sincere desire to rekindle the customer's interest.

Figure 2

Dear Mr. Wilson:

It suddenly hit me like a bolt from the blue this morning—I haven't seen you or heard from you in over three months—and you used to be one of our best customers! Maybe you were well stocked on all of our items and you are experiencing one of those "valleys of slow turnover" we all see, but it also occurred to me we might have done something to offend you!

I've heard it said somewhere: "There are many good excuses for losing an order, but none for losing good will." This I believe and it's why I'm writing you—not to find out if you're taking your business elsewhere—which is certainly your privilege—but to make sure it wasn't because of something we did which has lost us your good will, a most important asset to us.

If it is true that you have been buying your material elsewhere, we sincerely hope it gives you the service and performance you want at a reasonable price. We thank you for your past patronage and will always be glad to count you as one of our most valued customers and friends. However, if it is in reality something we said or did which lost us your good will, we would be most grateful indeed if you'd tell us about it. We're here to help you and to do everything in our power to bring you back into our family of satisfied customers.

Regardless of the reason, I would be most happy to hear from you at anytime in the near future to compare notes.

Sincerely,

A.B. Cummings

Let's stop for a minute and look at Mr. Cummings' letter:

Paragraph 1—Opening on a friendly, interested, and novel note. Shows a valid reason for writing and also your concern with the customer's feelings.

Paragraph 2—Stresses importance of good will to you and properly prepares the customer for the question.

Paragraph 3—Allows for the possibility the customer may have found a better supplier, wishes him well, and thanks him for his past business. Then turns the coin over and poses the other possibility that your company did something wrong which caused a breach. Offers an open door to the customer to discuss the problem and get things "back on the track" again.

Paragraph 4—Important psychological close to keep the door open for any outcome. Don't leave the customer with the impression you are only concerned with his business or friendship under certain terms.

In every business, there are customers who require special attention. Some should get it merely because the large volume of their business justifies every possible special or even personal consideration. Some customers may be merely demanding or eccentric, but who are we to judge? Their money is just as good as anyone else's.

ASSISTING A SALESMAN THROUGH LETTERS

Your salesman may be assisted, through letters, in two general ways. One type of letter prepares the ground for him; introduces him, mentions the new line he will demonstrate, some special offer he will explain, etc. The primary purpose for this letter is to introduce the salesman, not to substitute for his call. It should stimulate the customer's curiosity and leave it up to the salesman to satisfy it. This type of letter is exemplified in Figure 3.

Figure 3

Dear Mr. Hollister:

Thank you for your order of May 12. All of the items are in stock and should be delivered to you within the next few days.

As you know, Roy Merritt, who formerly covered your territory, is no longer with us. However, we have been fortunate in adding a new man, Mr. Carleton Alexander who, I am sure, will be able to look after you the way Roy did.

During the first month Carleton spent most of his time in the main office learning our product line. He impressed me as a sincere, honest, likeable type whom I feel sure you will like. He has had considerable experience in our line, so he is familiar with our operation and how it fits in with your needs.

Carleton will call on you during the week of May 25 with samples of some of our new products, which look better than ever. We've added a few novelty items and one or two revolutionary new concepts which, I am sure, will do well in your store. Be sure to ask him about them.

I am looking forward to an even better year with you than we enjoyed last year. Best wishes for a prosperous future.

Sincerely,

Russell Bennett

Another type of letter, written in a similar vein but with a different twist, will help to bring customers to your store or office. Letters sent to a customer between sales calls generally strengthen the salesman-customer relationship. This type of letter is seen in Figure 4. The purpose and approach used in each letter are almost self-evident.

Figure 4

Dear Mr. Sweeney:

When you visited our office last year, you left me with the impression you thoroughly enjoyed yourself and were looking forward to coming back in a short while. I'm sorry you haven't been able to visit us as you planned.

Even though our representative, Mr. Bradley Benedict, has enjoyed a pleasant and profitable relationship with your company during the past year, he feels there are some new and different styles which would be more impressive to you if you saw them first hand and on display. I tend to agree with him, so I am taking this opportunity to personally invite you to pay us another visit as soon as your schedule permits.

We have just added three more outstanding styles that I have personally examined and I have great confidence in—one dealer who tried them out sold two of them out in *three* days and the other one in *five* days. I could send pictures of them to you but you know photographs cannot do them justice—you have to see them in person to get the real impact.

I will be leaving on a buying trip in about ten days, so I hope you can see your way clear to visit us sometime before that—that way I can give you my undivided attention. Just call me and let me or my secretary know when to expect you. I will look forward to your visit.

Cordially,

Marshall Richards

Vice-President, Sales

It is well to point out a fact which might have been overlooked— the letters we have just discussed still retain the four elements so important to a successful sales letter:

- they are couched in *simple* terms. No long words or involved sentences are used;
- they are *novel*. Each one has a beginning designed to capture the reader's attention;

- they are *appealing* because the writer speaks in terms of the reader's needs, not his own; and
- for the most part, they are *provocative* because, in each case, some incentive has been added to coax the reader to take some kind of positive action. In other words, they still have S-N-A-P.

DIRECT SALES LETTERS

In the second category—the direct sales letter designed to sell a specific product, idea, or service—we begin to encounter a slightly different problem and approach, where the emphasis should be on the *benefits* of the product itself rather than any association with a salesman or a previous business connection.

The same general principles of structure apply in direct sales letters as in all business letters, but much greater latitude is allowed, just as greater latitude is allowed in the sales approach in general. You can be more imaginative, unconventional, and use more color, and, necessarily, use a certain amount of bragging. Normally, the conventional sales letter comprises six important parts. Let's take the format point by point:

Salutation: One of the main liberties you may take is with the salutation. In volume mailings, where use of an individual address is impractical, anonymous salutations such as "Dear Friend," "Dear Sir," or "Dear Madam" may be used. But the unusual is better, such as "To the Forward-Looking Businessman," or "To the Young Lady Who Has a Sharp Eye."

Opening: The most crucial part of a sales letter. It is the writer's bid for attention; if it fails, the whole effort is wasted. Some firms go to considerable trouble and expense to devise catchy, attention-getting openings. Devices like these, however, must be used with care. They are novelties and they don't always work. Even though they may appeal to some readers, they may annoy others.

Dramatic Opening: One tried and true method for getting attention is to put your opening in the form of a question. When you do this, you are taking advantage of a quirk of human nature. People always react to a question as a challenge, and it is a rare person who does not respond. A direct challenge is also a good type of opening, such as "You can have a Cadillac in your garage by sundown!" A third type of opening is the use of a well-known proverb, especially if it is turned around into an interesting twist.

Body: Having gained attention by your opening, in whatever form it may be, you must next keep the reader's interest while making sales points in the body of your letter. This may consist of many things, such as anecdotes, facts and figures, results of lab tests, consumption statistics, testimonials, guarantees, and any other inducements to get the reader to buy. The main part, or the "meat" of your message, should appear about *1/3rd* or *2/5ths* of the way down the letter, so that it comes into proper focus.

Close: As you all know, it used to be considered de rigueur to close letters with "hoping" or "trusting" or "I remain" and similar innocuous words, but they are not usually tolerated in modern communications. Sales letters now end with forceful suggestions for immediate action. They ask for the order, and they enforce it with all kinds of inducements to get action. Here the "you attitude" becomes important again. The seller takes care not to show his anxiety to make a sale, per se. What he stresses is the *buyer's* interests. The buyer will get a bargain, or he will be guaranteed against dissatisfaction in some form, such as the privilege of returning the merchandise, or payment will be made easy for him.

Postscript: Used to be frowned upon in business correspondence as being unacceptable in proper circles. Today, however, few sales letters are written without them. The postscript, however, has won general adoption because of the special services it may perform. It can remove from the body of the letter, where it might get lost, some special item which should be brought to the reader's attention.

An equally important aspect of sales letters is the letter written to sell a certain product. As stated earlier, the same rules apply as in other sales letters, but more attention and emphasis is placed on the specific, individual, and unusual qualities you product has to offer over the "run of the mill" variety. Figure 5 is a good example of this type of letter.

Figure 5

MILLER MENS WEAR

Coe, Illinois

April 7, 19___

Dear Friend:

How would you like to get a new pair of slacks practically without charge or obligation? You've never seen anything like this before . . . because there has never been a bargain quite like it!

For ONE WEEK ONLY we are offering a once-a-year deal on EVVA-LAST Slacks. EVVA-LAST Denim Slacks are a blend of Western styling in a rugged fabric of 50% Fortrel polyester and 50% cotton—proven by many recent tests to be more than *twice* as durable as ordinary fabric. EVVA-LAST Slacks combine durability with modern style.

Scoop front pockets, patch back pockets, and wide belt loops. Bartacked at all stress points, plus safety stitched seams for extra strength. Trim-Cut, designed primarily for the young man with a slim build (24" - 34" waist); or Trim-Regular Cut, designed for the man with an average build (over 34").

Machine washable, tumble dry. Maximum fabric shrinkage guaranteed not to exceed 2%! Offered in 6 exciting colors: Chocolate Brown, Desert Tan, Sky Blue, Navy Blue, Apple Green, and Burgundy.

The best part is the fantastic BARGAIN PRICE! Instead of our standard low price of $11.98 per pair, we offer them in this special sale for *only* $5.95 per pair or, better yet, *two* pair for only $9.96! That's a real saving, when you buy two pair, of $14.00!

Remember, this offer is good for SEVEN DAYS, so don't delay! Order two pair and save $14.00. Do yourself a favor—order four pair and save $28.00! It's a bargain we've never offered before and it's better than getting a new pair free!

Just tell us the style and color you want, your waist and inseam leg measurements on the handy enclosed card, and mail it back *today*. EVVA-LAST Slacks may be returned within 10 days for full refund if you are not satisfied. I'll rush your slacks to you post-haste. You'll be glad you acted now!

Sincerely,

Stan

Stan Brown

Sales Manager

Encl

Paragraph 1—An impressive and eye-catching opening. Any one of several could have been used, but this is an excellent approach, mainly because it implies something will be FREE.

Paragraph 2—States a brief but important part of the offer. Don't give the *whole* offer before telling the reader what he will get, however. Mention most salable features of your product, to whet and heighten the reader's interest.

Paragraphs 3 and 4—"Nut shell" statements as to what the product is, its style, material, and primary selling points. More impressive if not combined into one "heavy" paragraph. Try not to make paragraphs longer than 5 or 6 lines. Point out important features of the product, specifying those characteristics which combine to make that product outstanding, worth more than you are asking, or otherwise attractive. Every word should sell, help to make the product more desirable to the reader, or otherwise induce him to act. Make him *want* to own it!

Paragraph 5—States the price in such a way that it is a real, legitimate bargain. Gives reasons why it appears that way. Usually effective to compare it with something well known or comparable, or to refer to prices you would *expect* to pay for an item of the same quality, size or quantity. Headline the fact that it is a bargain. Usually a good idea to add an additional incentive, such as "Two for the price of one," etc.

Paragraphs 6 and 7—Encourages reader to act *now*. Always try to include a time limitation for taking advantage of the offer, or point out what will be lost if the reader fails to act. *Urgency* is of paramount importance in a sales letter.

Try to encourage more than one order if it is feasible. Give reader *specific* instructions on what he has to do to order; keep it *simple*, but don't leave out any essential details, such as warranties or guarantees you are offering.

IMPORTANCE OF FOLLOW-UP AND ANSWERS TO INQUIRIES

When enough time has elapsed for a new customer to have used and tested your products, it is a good idea to write to him and ask whether he is satisfied with the product. Also, it is wise to ask him if he has any suggestions to make. Letters of this type may bring testimonials that will prove extremely valuable in your promotion. You can build up an impressive testimonial file from the favorable letters you receive. You can also draw upon such a file when approaching prospects in the same area or in the same line.

Answers to inquiries are a major part of business correspondence. They can be the most important type of sales letter. Someone has gone to the trouble of looking you up in the yellow pages, or has been referred to you by a friend. He writes to you for information. His inquiry to you may be the only one he is making but, at the same time, he may be making the same inquiry of your competitor. You have no way of knowing. Therefore, you had better do your best to make your reply a sales letter and win his business.

Promptness is of the first importance, but directness is also important. Give specific answers to the questions. Being specific, however, does not mean being overly detailed. A good sales letter is organized to have a certain impact. Primarily, your letter should do two things:

1. Put the prospect into the buying mood; and

2. Whet his interest so that he will want to look into details.

These appeals can be furnished in an attractive and effective brochure. However, avoid the "clutter" of too much literature. Experience has shown that, beyond a certain point, more can become "too much." Enclosures should not overshadow the letter.

Once again we should pause for a few moments to refresh our memory. The second category of letters, just like the third, must retain the four elements of successful sales letters which were outlined in the beginning, i.e., they are all written in simple terms, they have novel openings, they have appeal because the reader's interest is paramount, and they are provocative because the reader is impelled to take action which promises to be profitable to both parties. As we have intimated many times, a sales letter will end up in the wastebasket if it doesn't have S-N-A-P

MAIL-ORDER SALES

We should, of course, say a few words about the first category—mail-order sales. What has been said in the past about sales letters in general applies, of course, to the mail-order sales campaign, except that such campaigns have special features and problems peculiar to that type.

Although not as big a part of the American scene as it used to be, mail-order sales remain one of its biggest businesses. People, however, should be aware of certain developments that have taken place. For example, the farm population has declined from about 50% to less than 20% of the national total. On the other side of the coin, big city department stores, following their customers to the suburbs, have picked up many of the farmer shoppers.

Mail-order market specialists, therefore, have had to show alertness and ingenuity to meet this challenge. Companies like Sears, Spiegel, etc., continue to send out millions of catalogs. To a marked degree, mail-order sales is a field in itself and requires the talents of an experienced person to adequately run a campaign and produce results.

Another advantage of direct mail is its flexibility. Through careful testing, every element in the campaign can be validated beforehand to assure the best returns. Necessary changes can be made. Still another advantage is economy. On a large variety of products, mailing and other costs are considerably less than dealer's discounts and direct salesmens' commissions.

Three things you should know to be a good mail-order copywriter:

1. Know what you are selling. Study the article or the service carefully. Know it thoroughly before you write about it. The better you know it, the better able you will be to choose your selling points, to write with "feel" and conviction about them.
2. Know your market. What is the income level that is to be appealed to? How do current economic conditions affect your potential customers' buying habits?
3. Know the prospect. Study the lists you use. Such things as age, sex, or locality all influence buying habits and trends.

You will find that most good sales letters use more than one appeal. The bargain appeal may be enhanced by stressing quality, and vice versa. Other inducements are usually added to break down sales resistance. It is good policy to offer a variety of inducements.

CUSTOMER MOTIVES TO WHICH YOU SHOULD APPEAL

A distinguished psychologist has given the following as most of the motives to which the sales-letter writer can appeal:

Appetite—hunger	Possession	Rest—sleep
Love of offspring	Approval of others	Home comfort
Health	Gregariousness	Economy
Sex attraction	Respect for Deity	Curiosity
Parental affection	Taste	Efficiency
Ambition	Personal appearance	Competition
Pleasure	Safety	Cooperation
Bodily comfort	Cleanliness	Virility

Try to concentrate the mail appeal in a single phrase or sentence. If you do this, you can use it as an opening sentence and re-use it, possibly with an interesting variation, in the body of the letter.

Additional appeals in mail-order campaigns usually take the form of supplementary inducements. For example, the writer may point out the small number of purchasers to whom the offer is made. For another thing, the words BARGAIN PRICE or ONE WEEK ONLY in heavy type on an order form will pull many more inquiries than the same form without it.

A mail order campaign may rely only on sales letters; it may depend upon an advertising campaign, in which mailings are coordinated with various forms of advertising. In any case, whatever form it takes, it should never be treated as an insignificant detail.

Care should be taken, if the order form is part of other printed matter, to *set it off* by some means. Essentials of the order form include the firm name, address, zip code, and key number to denote the source of the order, such as the initials of the magazine.

If the order form is to consummate a sale, the specifications should then be *clearly* stated—conditions under which a refund is guaranteed, time limit for the return of merchandise, method of remittance, postage and handling costs, tax, etc.

Following is a brief summary of the various types of direct mail:

- the sales letter, which has been discussed.
- the post card. May be white or light-colored stock and may be printed on both sides.
- the leaflet. A single sheet printed on one or both sides, in one or more colors.
- the circular. A printed piece that may be folded, usually in two or four colors.
- the broadside. A mailing piece which is unusual in shape, size, or manner of folding.
- the self-mailer. A folded sheet of sturdy paper, thereby making envelopes unnecessary.
- the brochure or catalog. A more elaborate form of circular, more attractive, but more expensive & usually more productive.

SIX RULES FOR LETTERS THAT SELL

We could probably sum it all up by stating there are six general rules for writing letters that sell. They are:

1. *Qualify.* A letter is often a substitute for a personal visit or a salesman. Know your prospect. No sales letter should ever be written until you have determined that the people your letter is aimed at are truly potential buyers.

2. *Identify.* Limit the scope. Every letter has a purpose to sell a *specific* product, service, or idea. Don't confuse the issue or the reader with unrelated information or data.

3. *Organize.* The effective sales letter format has 5 points:

a. Introduces itself by gaining favorable *attention* at the start. This is where Novelty is so important.

b. Shows the article by illustration, sample, or both.

c. *Prices* the article plainly.

d. Describes the *advantages* of owning the article so attractively the reader has an irresistible urge to buy. Do not be afraid to write long letters, if it takes a long letter to tell your story properly.

e. Urges the reader to *act at once.* Stresses immediate action, because readers are prone to delay, rationalize, or forget.

4. *Vitalize.* Be convincing. Sell yourself first. Gain confidence by what you say and how you say it. Use short words and short sentences to get your point across.

5. *Humanize.* Be original. Use your imagination. It is your imagination that makes your letters different—gives an interesting approach, creates desire, or helps illustrate a point.

6. *Dramatize.* Instead of saying, for example, "This pipe is treated for proper temperature and humidity," why not say "No need to break this pipe in every time you want to 'fire up.' Nor do you have to leave it in a humidifier or any special place inbetween."?

In the final analysis, your approach is limited only by the extent and ingenuity of your imagination, and the appeal you use should be tailored to fit the occasion. This is well illustrated in Figure 6, an example of a letter sent to guests, who at one time or another had stayed at the Hotel Carlton, and management wanted to encourage them to return at their next opportunity.

Figure 6

September 29, 19__

HOTEL CARLTON * DALLAS

Dear Mr. Foster:

Last night I barbecued a chicken on the roof of Hotel Carlton!

After a year of eating perfect, aged roast beef in the Rib Room and gourmet dishes in the Rendezvous, I just needed a change.

But unless you plan to stay a year with us (which gets to be a little steep at $4,380., based on our $12.00 single room price), I don't think you'd ever get too much of our delicious food. Or our personal service.

Like I keep telling you, we're a very lovable hotel. With great treats planned for you when you do come stay with us, like:

> Room service is going to bring you a complimentary newspaper with your breakfast
>
> Reservations is going to put you in a beautiful room with a nice view of our park and plaza
>
> Airport limousine service is going to drive you here, non-stop, on the double
>
> The bell captain is going to let you use his private putter on our 18-hole green

And I'd liketo have you up for barbecued chicken, but the chef would flatten me for sure.

Cordially,

James C. Grove

Vice President and General Manager

P.S. Oh yes—the Boss wants to give you a cigaret lighter with your monogram on it. Would you like that?

8

How To Write Effective
Credit Letters

Jason Pollard, Credit Manager for a large Department store in Detroit many years ago told me, "Those guys upstairs can write all the letters they want but I don't want any of them to write to any of *my* accounts!"

When I asked why, he added, "Because, whether you realize it or not, credit letters require a completely different psychology than a straight business letter."

Further discussion with him soon made me realize exactly what the basic difference was between the two. In the ordinary business or sales letter, the whole concept is motivational. In other words, you want the reader to buy a product, a service, an idea, or you want him to agree with you.

On the other hand, in the credit as well as the collection letter, the controlling influence is monetary. People either *owe* you money, or they *want* money or its equivalent. Everything else revolves around that principle. Unfortunately, there are very few people in business today who are not faced with one big problem: How do I collect my acconts receivable and not lose a customer?

The fractured prayer of the credit manager: "Forgive us this day our debtors..." gives rise to the question: Are all delinquent accounts deadbeats? I would say it's very doubtful. As a matter of fact, extensive analysis of many accounts receivables has shown quite the contrary. Instances of real crooks—those who never intend to pay—are quite rare. Most debtors fall into one of three categories:

1. The biggest class of debtors are too immature or too uninformed to handle their own affairs. They commit themselves to pay for more than they can.

2. Another big class of debtors just doesn't realize that it is morally wrong not to pay.

3. The third class are intelligent and moral but go into the hole for some good reason and then get panicked.

The credit process in a business relationship begins with either an oral or written request for credit, and ends either with payment or with letters asking for payment of overdue bills or, if necessary, cancelling the credit privileges. Regardless of the outcome, the Credit Department has a tremendous responsibility.

The credit relationship between any two people, or an individual and a company, usually floats on the "Four C's":

- Capital
- Capacity
- Character
- Conditions

Capital, of course, represents the value of a person's assets; capacity shows his ability to pay; character demonstrates his integrity and willingness to pay; and conditions are the general business and economic conditions which prevail at the time.

With the many credit agencies available today, verifying credit is not too difficult a task. Information can be readily obtained from such large credit agencies as Dun and Bradstreet, from confidential reports of bankers or other financial or loan institutions, or from the local credit bureau.

You would want, of course, each one of the "Four C's" to be satisfactory. If this were always true, credit would not be a risky business. However, most people do well to meet three out of four. If a person pays his bills faithfully and usually on time, he has earned the right to be considered a good risk.

Experience has shown that the great majority of American people are honest and trustworthy. This does not mean, however, that you can afford to give everyone a line of credit just because he asks for it. More than anything else it means that the credit manager should give the applicant the benefit of the doubt until he proves he can't handle it.

The value of learning how to write credit letters is that you will have a unique opportunity to exercise your judgment and tact as well as to demonstrate your ability to communicate with other people in an area that very few understand or even like to try their hand at.

Developing credit accounts doesn't always result from a request from a potential buyer. In fact, there are two types of letters which have become almost a standard part of business operation: (i) the letter written to solicit new business, and (ii) the letter written to motivate those who have been qualified as good credit risks but have failed to exercise the privilege.

SEVEN STEPS TO MOTIVATE DORMANT CREDIT ACCOUNTS

Usually these types of letters are written by retail or department stores to old customers or good prospects who have been checked out. Each letter, of course, will have to be custom tailored to fit the individual or a group. Within this framework of prospects, the following general rules apply:

1. Catch the reader's interest. It's no good at all if they don't at least read it!
2. Use either a class appeal ("everybody's doing it") or the reverse psychology ("you have been selected . . .").
3. Highlight a major advantage to encourage him to continue reading.
4. State a brief reason for the letter. Show the intent and the advantage in providing the service.
5. Show what you have already done for the prospect.
6. Point out all the advantages of using the credit privilege.
7. Close with an invitation to action. Make it easy to do.

Figure 1 is an example of this kind of letter.

Figure 1

Dear Mr. Foley:

There's something I would like to show you if it were practical for me to be there in person. But, since I can't be there, I hope you will bear with me for a moment.

Were you aware that you have a good line of credit at Bellinghams already established? I'm sure you are aware of the convenience of simply saying, "Charge it!"

We felt sure you would enjoy this special service, to reap the benefits of its many advantages—that is why we took the liberty of opening an account for you.

Many women find, and I'm sure you will agree—a charge account really simplifies shopping. No need to be home to pay C.O.D. bills, you don't have to carry a lot of money, and it saves you time besides. Now isn't that an offer that's hard to resist?

Let us show you how easy it is. The next time you are down this way, just present the enclosed card and say, "Charge it, please!"

Sincerely,

John Brown

Encl

Then, of course, there are always a few people who take the trouble to get a credit account established and, for some reason, seldom if ever use it. In order to incite these people to action, most companies send out reminders—all the way from a small 4" X 6" card to a long, pleasingly toned, letter. It's up to the credit manager how much time he feels he can afford to devote to these types to rekindle their purchasing spirit.

The customer may never actually look at it this way, and the credit manager may not either, but the customer is in reality doing the creditor a favor when he applies for credit. He is a *brand new customer* and the company's reaction should be *positive* rather than *negative*. Figure 2 is a sample acknowledgement of a request.

Figure 2

September 20, 19___

Dear Mr. Hamilton:

Thank you for your letter of September 17. We would like very much to be of service to you and your company.

As you are aware, we must of course process a routine credit check. This should not be any more than a mere formality, a matter of a few days.

We hope this delay will not inconvenience you. If you have a need to order something within the next day or two, we would like to suggest you fill out and return the C.O.D. order form we have provided for you. We will be glad to serve you on either a cash, check, or COD basis until the credit verification procedure is complete.

Thank you again for your inquiry and we anticipate a long and profitable business relationship.

Sincerely,

Allan Beard

Encl

It isn't always necessary to acknowledge a request for credit as a separate issue. If the credit bureau, bank or other reference point is close enough to verify by telephone, then the acknowledgement and the credit approval can be combined. Your reply should be all on the positive side, warm, friendly, and outgoing, and should answer all questions the customer raised in his request.

You should also cover your company's credit terms and total time allowed for repayment of bills, give a general pitch on the products and services your company offers, and close your letter in a warm and friendly manner.

Of course, if the prospect merely requested a line of credit but did not say anything about a specific order, your reply would be responsive primarily to the request for credit, but it should also add a line something like: "We sincerely appreciate having the opportunity to serve you and we are looking forward to a long, friendly, and profitable relationship."

REFUSING A REQUEST FOR CREDIT

Sometimes it is necessary to refuse a request for credit. This, as you would assume, requires a little tact and diplomacy. You want to do business with this person, but you can't afford to run the risk of granting him a line of credit.

The applicant must be made to realize four things:

1. He must pay cash or C.O.D. for what he orders.
2. He must always be made to feel that you would grant him the credit if it were practical to do so.
3. You will extend the credit privilege as soon as you can.
4. You value him as a customer *just as much* by his being a cash customer as you would if he were a credit customer.

While there are many variations, following is an example of a refusal that was accepted by the prospect in the proper way:

Dear Mr. Galloway:

Thank you for your nice letter of January 12. We are glad to have the opportunity to be of service to you and we appreciate the credit information you supplied.

The credit references you gave us were cooperative and straight forward and verified what you had indicated to us. Analysis of your financial capabilities and reports from our credit agencies, however, indicate that adding another obligation at this particular time may create somewhat of a hardship for you. Your cash flow does not appear to be strong enough to properly liquidate all your commitments in a timely manner. We have therefore decided to postpone granting a line of credit to you for the time being.

In spite of this decision, however, we wish to emphasize that this is a temporary position on our part and we sincerely want to do business with your company. We feel you have a very promising potential and we want to be a part of it. We would like to suggest, therefore, that you place an order for what you feel you can handle on a cash, check or COD basis.

We would also like to point out that buying for cash in small quantities has many advantages:

- You will have clean, fresh stock on your shelves.
- You will realize a more rapid turnover.
- You will be building a foundation for a line of credit with us in the near future.
- You will get the 2% discount for cash on all purchases.
- Delivery charges will be prepaid.
- You will get more prompt delivery.

Be assured, Mr Galloway whether it's for cash or on credit, your business will always be appreciated. You will receive prompt service and we will be anxious to add you to our list of credit customers at the earliest opportunity.

Sincerely,

Jason Forbes

Once the credit check has been made and the customer is on a firm credit footing, the regular business relationship is established. From this point forward, except for the regular sales promotion programs, the maintenance and development of that relationship is chiefly the responsibility of the credit manager.

IMPORTANCE OF A CREDIT SALES DEPARTMENT

It is quite obvious that most businesses these days rely on credit sales for a large percentage of their business. In some cases, it has gone over 90%. Many of them have said, "I couldn't have survived without the credit purchaser. And my losses are not really that great that I have to worry about it."

Many successful businessmen are willing to promote, screen, and merchandise new charge accounts. They have established a credit sales promotion department, and they say "thank you" to their cash sales customers, mail order customers, as well as newcomers.

The primary function of a credit sales promotion department is to write warm, personal and appealing letters; and sell the customer on the store, product or service and credit facilities. It also tries to continue to promote friendly feelings; demonstrate good will; solicit charge account customers; reactivate good-paying, high-limit customers that have been lost; keep good customers; and secure new customers.

A satisfied charge customer is one of your best salesmen. She will sell her friends. Word of mouth advertising, more frequently than not, is one of the best forms of advertising. In addition, a "thank you" letter is always in good taste, spreads good will, and may even revive a semi-dormant account.

Maintaining and promoting credit accounts is an important function for many companies. Many times a follow up letter to a dormant credit account has divulged a customer who was turned away because of some minor dissatisfaction. The letter brought it to light and saved not only that customer but others who had noticed the same thing.

There are many ways to approach a dormant account, most of them good. The important thing is to be brief, sincere and use down-to-earth language. Following is but one example:

Dear Mr. Herman:

Forgive me for not writing sooner, but I just noticed we haven't had an order from you or heard from you in almost three months.

I have been sitting here wracking my brains trying to figure out what we have done to cause this. Maybe it's because of something one of our clerks or sales force said that upset you.

In any event, I would like you to call me or write and tell me the reason. I will be only too happy to have the opportunity to make it right, whatever the reason may be. You are always welcome and it will be a pleasure to serve you.

Sincerely,

Frank Seymour

CRITICAL POINTERS ABOUT CREDIT CUSTOMERS

A few words should be added to what we have already said about credit customers before going on to collection letters:

• A complete explanation of store policy and terms should be provided when the account is opened. The customer is new and does not understand all the rules and regulations you have been working under. If he or she has any questions or doubts, this is the time to bring them up and clarify them.

• If a customer is dissatisfied, *listen.* If an adjustment proves to be necessary, make it. Nothing will turn away a good customer quicker than to be given the feeling that "no one gives a darn." If he gets this impression, he will not only leave your store disgruntled and unhappy, but he is almost sure to tell his friends. This could be serious.

• Bill each customer promptly and correctly. Everyone likes to know where he stands on his "end of the month" bill session. If he or she doesn't know what he owes you and isn't sure that you know either, he will begin to lose confidence in you and that only means he will stop trading with you.

• A large percentage of inactive charge accounts land in the "paid-up graveyard" due to neglect. Send them a statement with a word or two about missing the opportunity of serving them better. If this doesn't work, write them a letter. They will almost always respond in one way or another. At least a woman will be flattered to know you care about her. The customer who is now inactive was once considered to be a good credit risk. He is also human. Treat him like one and you will be surprised how many times it will bring him back.

Remember, business profits are based on *satisfied* customers.

9

Writing Collection Letters That Get the Job Done

For every bright side, of course, there is a darker side. Unfortunately, this is only too true in the credit business. However, we all have to face the real world—the real world that doesn't pay its bills on time.

A collection letter is a unique business letter. Whether you think about the other kinds in these terms, this one can truly be called a "type." The reason it differs from other letters is that it *has* to do the job—it must *collect the money*.

As anyone knows, it is no easy job to collect overdue bills. A credit manager has the two-fold problem of changing a completely negative message into a positive one, and also collecting the money.

Most people who are shirking their responsibility have an inner awareness of it and have developed some sort of defense mechanism about it, or have rationalized their action one way or another. This is especially true of those people who have failed to pay their bills.

THE TIME-TESTED "COLLECTION SERIES" LETTERS

This phenomenon is one of the main reasons why the so-called "collection series" of letters was developed. The credit man is obliged to remind the debtor that he has failed to pay but, at the same time, he cannot afford to label all "slow pay" customers as deadbeats. He will not only run the risk of losing a customer but inviting a lawsuit as well.

The collection series most generally followed consists of five letters or memos:

1. A statement of account—with or without a comment. This is a gentle reminder to the debtor calling his attention to a matter of fact. It does not assume anything except perhaps an oversight.
2. A brief letter or friendly note, recapping what you want to say and giving the customer the benefit of the doubt.
3. A longer, more formal, letter outlining the importance of prompt payment of the bill and asking for some overt action on the part of the debtor to liquidate his indebtedness.
4. A letter asking for specific, timely steps the debtor can take or will agree to follow to pay off his bill. Usually asks for the debtor to write, phone or visit the creditor to resolve the mutual problem.
5. Seldom used except by certain collection agencies. This letter threatens cancellation of the debtor's credit privileges and/or possible legal action.

The brief note (no. 2 above) need only cover three essential points:

- the reason for the note (such as "We have not received your last payment for _____").
- "Save Face" psychology ("Perhaps you overlooked sending your last payment . . .").
- Apology and close. (Such as "If you have sent the payment in this month, please disregard this reminder and accept our thanks for taking care of it.")

By the time the account gets around to the need for the third letter, the Credit Manager has to begin to apply a little pressure. It is no longer a case of somebody forgetting to do something. It is a clear case of intent on the part of the debtor not to pay—at least not on time.

The big problem is: it might be strictly a case of one-time failure on his part, and the credit man cannot afford to throw it all away on one false assumption. Or, worse yet, it may be a failure on the part of the company and the customer is nursing a grievance. In any event, it behooves the credit manager to get to the real cause of the problem without offending the customer. Here is a sample letter of this type:

Dear Mr. Parsons:

Our records indicate, as shown on the attached statement, that you owe us $250.55. Does this account agree with yours? We realize, of course, it is possible you have withheld paying on this account because of some error we have made or some faulty merchandise you may have received. Perhaps some adjustment one of our clerks failed to make. If this has happened, please let us know at once so we can rectify the mistake right away. We regret any inconvenience it may have caused you.

However, if there is nothing wrong, we hasten to point out your account is over three months in arrears. As you know, good credit is an extremely valuable asset. I'm sure you'd want to protect it and we sincerely want to help you do so.

We can't help you resolve the problem, whatever it is, unless we know what it is. Our doors are always open. Please call or write and let us know why we haven't heard from you or, if you feel you can, mail us your check today.

Sincerely,

John Quincy, Credit Manager

A variation of the above, and one that is used often by many companies, is for the credit manager to allow or suggest a series of smaller payments--say three or four--instead of payment all at one time. Here again, it depends on the type of customer, the credit policy of the company, and the size of the bill.

Occasionally a credit stall gets around to the "eleventh hour" class, or the next to the last resort letter--asking for specific steps a debtor will follow to liquidate a debt. The credit manager is almost committed to threaten the debtor with drastic action to get results. He will, of course, be friendly, but he must be patient and at the same time completely frank about the whole matter. Following is a good example:

Attention: Carl Kincaid

Dear Carl:

We have been friends for a long time—long enough for me to feel I can lay my cards on the table and expect that you will do the same. I don't want you to feel, Carl, I am trying to use strong-arm tactics because you have owed us over $450.00 for almost six months.

Up until this year you have always paid your bills on time—in some cases ahead of time—that is commendable—so I can't help but feel you are having some kind of financial problem that makes it difficult for you to clear things up. I'm not prying—I don't want to get into your personal affairs. I'm not really concerned with *how* it happened, but I am concerned with how I can help you get *out* of the problem. If we can't turn to our good friends in time of need, who can we turn to?

I would be kidding you, Carl, if I told you we don't want the money. Of course we do. But we also want to keep both your business and your friendship, and I'm sure we can accomplish all three things if we work together.

All I want you to do is to call me or, if you prefer, write me a personal letter in strict confidence and explain it in full. If it is a matter of shortness of cash, I'm sure we can work out a convenient payment schedule for you without undue hardship. We may even be able to continue to supply your business needs at the same time until you get back on a firmer footing.

Carl, I'm being frank with you. All I want or expect is for you to level with me, O.K.? If you will use the enclosed envelope, your reply will come directly to me.

Cordially,

Hal Prince

The foregoing is a "this is your last chance—you'd better lay it on the line" type of letter. There is nothing much more can be said. But why did we write it this way?

Paragraph 1: Start off with a friendly approach. You want him to read the letter and answer it, not "point your finger" at and antagonize him. Make him feel you at least are willing to play ball, at the same time mentioning the reason for the letter.

Paragraph 2: Comment on his good past record and why you have confidence in his desire to pay his bill. If you don't trust him, how can you get him to trust you?

Paragraphs 3 and 4: Turn the problem around and show how you want to work together to resolve it but, above all, be sincere and believable. Keep the friendly approach.

Paragraph 5: Show reader how easy it is to call or write and take a big step toward resolving his problem. Encourage him to contact you—that's what's important.

Paragraph 6: Good "fair deal" arrangement between friends. Also, re-emphasize the security of the discussion by writing directly to you.

The fifth and last letter, as stated before, is seldom used except by collection agencies. Some companies hate to resort to this step because it is distasteful. It presents an ultimatum and, sometimes, the long-delinquent debtor is a good customer of long standing who has meant a lot of money, but how is having some temporary difficulties.

If the bill is of sufficient size, legal action is usually threatened and carried out. If, on the other hand, it is not large enough to warrant such action, the credit privilege is withdrawn. In either event, however, the credit manager should not be completely negative in his letter.

He should leave the door open for continuation of the business relationship—obviously on a cash or C.O.D. basis. Following is an example of this type of letter, tailored to fit a customer-creditor relationship:

March 17, 19___

Dear Mr. Tovar:

Our Credit Manager, Mr. Toomey, has referred your overdue account to me for permission to institute legal action. You are more than six months past due and all previous letters we have sent you have been unanswered.

Even though the record looks incriminating, I cannot accept the fact that you are purposely refusing to pay off your indebtedness. I have found many times that a customer wanted to continue doing business with our company, but was too embarrassed to discuss the fact that he had personal problems which prevented or seriously limited his payments.

I have also found, when both parties have a sincere desire to reach an amicable settlement, there is usually a way to work it out. Assuming this is true, we have only to sit down together to negotiate an agreement.

Company rules prevent me from granting you more than seven days to contact me and set up a conference. If I have not heard from you by March 24, appropriate legal steps, of course, must be taken.

Sincerely,

John Carmody, Vice-President

Some comments we should make about this letter:

Paragraph 1: A simple matter-of-fact statement regarding the facts of the case.

Paragraphs 2 and 3: In spite of the fact this is the fifth letter, it is not necessarily a good idea to give up completely. In this case, Mr. Carmody is providing Mr. Tovar one more opportunity to get in touch with him and work something out.

Paragraph 4: Even though Mr. Carmody is leaving the door open for Mr. Tovar to settle his account, he must put a deadline on how long he can leave it open. In addition to giving the debtor a specific deadline date, he used the passive rather than the active voice. The active voice: "I will take appropriate legal action . . ." in this case sounds too threatening and would probably defeat whatever chance you might have of securing cooperation.

TIPS FOR A GOOD CREDIT MANAGER

A good credit manager is a firm believer that most everyone will pay if given the opportunity. A good collector is like a good doctor—his real purpose is not to amputate, but to cure the infection. If the amputation is necessary, then it should be done quickly and cleanly.

If the customer makes a partial payment, it is evident he is trying. So, you should acknowledge the payment with thanks and ask him to write, phone, or stop in to arrange some method of taking care of the balance, to keep his credit good.

The few who don't respond must be handled as individual problems. Telephone or personal contact is often recommended. Never, however, in the handling of delinquent accounts, is harshness justified. A credit manager who doesn't believe in and like people is just in the wrong business.

From the 90-day-past-due stage on, use typed form and personal letters. A good form letter, neatly typed, will out-pull the average dictated letter, simply because the former is usually more carefully thought out.

It is also important to remember that *prompt* and *regular* collection follow-up is necessary. Don't make the mistake of letting a debtor get too far behind in his account or you are creating additional problems.

Write form letters to cover repetitive situations. Study every word closely. Make certain your meanings are clear. Don't threaten (until you reach the fifth stage). Don't use tricky, cute, or funny letters. Be businesslike, firm but fair.

SUBJECTIVE SATISFACTIONS OF CREDIT BUYERS

It is a good idea to periodically test your collection form letters: one to one group, one to another, and then check the results. People usually pay bills because of *subjective* satisfactions rather than for objective reasons (because it's due). In other words, *emotional reactions* to suggestion is the notivating force. Some of these subjective satisfactions are:

1. People generally want to do the right thing.
2. They want to be fair.
3. They want to be good citizens.
4. They want to keep credit facilities available to them.
5. They don't want it known they have a bad credit rating.
6. They were trained to regard bills as important.

Remember one of the truisms of the credit business: *Indifference* is the principal reason why customers quit. This may point to discourteous treatment, poor service, neglect, or all of them. You can't afford to let this factor or attitude dominate your day to day operation.

People yearn to be appreciated. They love individual attention; they seek recognition. A five-letter campaign once reactivated *48 percent* of inactive accounts. That credit manager realized the true importance of *soul* in his dealings with the public!

10

How to Write Letters That Satisfy Angry Customers

No matter which side you are on—the claimant or the "claimee"—if I'm permitted to coin a new word—it is money in your pocket. Whether you are trying to get recompensed for some product which failed to work, or trying to avoid replacing that product for an aggrieved customer, you are endeavoring to earn or save money. Either way, to know how to write a winning claim means money for you.

A famous department store in New York has long believed "the customer is always right," and will accept almost anything as returned merchandise in order to maintain good will. It also believes it is cheaper to keep an old customer than to acquire a new one. In this way, it is able to keep customers happy, contented and active.

The more automated that companies get and, consequently, the more dependent on the machine we become, the greater chance there is for machine-generated errors to occur. A product fails to function properly or not at all, a mistake is made in packing, crating, labelling, or in billing for the merchandise, or the wrong item is shipped. Many, many things can happen.

A customer writes to register a complaint and the recipient is faced with a decision. Is the complaint legitimate and, if so, what kind of an adjustment should be made?

It would perhaps be more accurate to say: the customer is *usually* right. There are many causes for customer complaints. You should always find out what they are. Complaints are like pains; they are danger signals for *action*. Every complaint letter you receive holds immense potential for good or bad. It should not be answered in a routine fashion by inexperienced personnel.

In reading a complaint letter, a company should consider the high cost of adjustment delay. The *longer* you wait to make an adjustment, the more business and money you will lose. The person making the complaint is already "hot under the collar," and unnecessary delay will only make things worse for all concerned.

Claim letters encompass a wide range of possible grievances. Hard and fast rules cannot be laid down to cover them all; therefore, we can only deal primarily with broad, general rules. The purpose of this chapter is to show you how to write effective claim letters and, for those of you who receive them, how to answer them so that the company's position is protected and the customer is reasonably satisfied.

CONSIDERATIONS EACH SIDE SHOULD HAVE IN A CLAIM

Just like any other area of communication, a claim is a two-way street. Neither side is always right nor, for that matter, is it always wrong. Every claimant should:

- Have a legitimate, or what he believes to be legitimate, complaint to write about.
- Be courteous and considerate, no matter how angry he may be. No one believes an angry man.
- Be able to prove his case within bounds of reason and in a timely manner.
- Have the right to a quick and equitable adjustment, if his claim is valid.
- Have the right to feel aggrieved for the inconvenience or the mistake, even if no adjustment is given.

On the other hand, the recipient of a claim letter has to:

- Be courteous, patient, and tactful.
- Be open-minded, fair, and reasonable.
- Be willing to take the time to find the cause and the extent of the complaint.
- Make an apology and an equitable adjustment if the claim proves to be a valid one.

- React in a reasonable period of time.
- Provide a full explanation of the reason behind a denial, if a complaint is not valid or an adjustment cannot be made.

If you are trying to write an effective claim letter, there are generally four important areas or points you should cover:

1. State *where* the error occurred and *who* is responsible. It simplifies and speeds up the verification procedure.

2. Motivate the reader by clearly spelling out the need for early action on his part. If it is truly urgent, you would probably telephone the reader to acquaint him with the facts as well as to impress on him the urgency of the problem and then confirm the call in writing.

3. Try to place the responsibility for the cost of returning the goods on the reader. If the vendor has really been at fault in some way in generating the claim action, then he should logically pay for the return of the merchandise.

4. What you consider a fair adjustment.

The above approach is the only logical one to use if you are trying to communicate with the average businessman. Putting the shoe on the other foot for a moment, what would be your reaction if you owned or managed a store and received this letter?

Dear Sir:

That color T.V. you told me was so great last week should have never come out of the carton. I can't get the picture to stop turning over and when I do I can't get the faces straight. Besides the color isn't dark enough.

Your repairman came out twice and adjusted it but he didn't help it much. I think you knew it was a lemon when you sold it to me. Well, you can come and get the thing and I'm through trading at your store.

Sincerely, Joe Campbell

The natural reaction to stupid mistakes is anger or, at least, displeasure but, if we stop to consider (1) we all make mistakes, and (2) 99 chances out of 100 it wasn't intentional, we will either forgive or, at least, be tolerant. It is to your advantage to be tolerant and in control of your emotions in your claim letter. If you are, your chances of gaining a fair and equitable adjustment are greatly increased.

With regard to the actual amount of the adjustment you want, it has been found to be generally the wisest policy to let the reader suggest a satisfactory settlement. He will ordinarily grant more than the customer would ask.

For a study in contrasts, consider the tone and makeup of the following letter as opposed to the previous letter:

April 11, 19____

Dear Sir:

On your March statement to me, I was charged $39.95 for a clock radio which I bought from your store on December 12. This bill was paid on January 11 by my check No. 426 on the Security Pacific National Bank, which cancelled check I received with my bank statement on February 7.

I received your statement in February and again in March showing $39.95 still unpaid. Would you please see that this payment is credited to my account so that this will not happen again? Thanking you in advance, I remain

Sincerely yours,

Steven Daniels

Do you think you would comply with his wishes?

Quick and courteous acknowledgment of claims is not only good public relations, but it is good business as well. In addition to showing your sincere concern for the customer's plight, you also establish certain facts concerning communications between you and your customer if it ever became a legal matter. Of course, you hope it never comes to that.

In acknowledging claim letters, the writer should, like the writer of a claim, cover four important areas:

1. Indicate by your wordage you are genuinely concerned about the writer's complaint and have some sympathy for his distress.

2. Assure the writer that his claim will be taken care of as quickly as possible without promising anything.

3. Furnish instructions, if appropriate, as to what the customer should do. For example, if an inspection is involved, who should do it, when and where it should be accomplished, and how it should be done so the customer will not have to suffer any additional expense, delay, or inconvenience as a result.

4. Try to get the writer to understand the reason for the delay and to be patient for a final and satisfactory answer.

One word of advice: before you acknowledge a claim letter from anyone, be sure to study the letter carefully. Make certain you understand completely and exactly what is involved. Find the meaning behind the words. You can't afford to "go off on a tangent" laboring under false assumptions or attacking the wrong problem. Furthermore, as mentioned earlier in discussing the tone of a claimant's letter, don't lose control of your emotions. Righteous indignation does not help customer relations. You may find it will help your emotional satisfaction, but it won't help your business.

They say there are three policies in effect concerning the granting of claims, but I don't believe the third one really exists. They are:

1. The "customer is always right" policy. As mentioned earlier, some firms still practice it.

2. Make a fair and equitable adjustment, depending on the merits of the case.

3. The "let the buyer beware" policy. I fail to see how any reputable firm can continue to operate on this one. If practiced avidly, this policy would soon drive all customers away.

APPROACH TO ADJUSTMENT LETTERS

The writer of an adjustment letter must be aware of the fact he is handling a delicate situation. The claimant is angry and convinced that your company is either crooked, inefficient, or both. Therefore, he feels he has a real legitimate grievance.

The object of the adjuster is three-fold: (i) to placate the irate customer, (ii) to make him see that the adjuster is trying to be fair, and (iii) to navigate carefully between two extreme positions: (a) agreeing too readily with the claimant, thus making him believe his claim is greater or better than he thought; and (b) being argumentative or accusing the customer of filing an unjust claim.

If the adjuster knows or is convinced the claim is valid and the customer is right, he has a built-in opportunity. The company has a contact with the customer that it would not otherwise have had. The writer should capitalize on it.

Replies to claim letters will accomplish one of three things:

1. Grant the adjustment requested;

2. Make an adjustment, but somewhat less than the customer requested; or

3. Refuse to make any adjustment.

In replying to claim letters where you feel the claim is valid and you are going to accede to the customer's wishes, you should:

- Thank the customer for returning the product as quickly as possible to avoid further damage, or cost, or other complications.
- Advise the customer that the claim is being granted. Explain what went wrong as well as you can and what is being done about it.
- Sell or resell the customer on your company's ability to continue to make quality products, in order to keep him as a customer.
- Remind the reader you are still interested in serving him as a customer in spite of what went wrong.

The points may be arranged to suit the customer, but your reply should be brief and sincere, as shown in Figure 1.

Figure 1

Dear Mr. Santoro:

We were very sorry to hear that the Ferranti Hi-Fi Equipment you purchased from us last week was not up to your expectations. Not only is this line of components exceptionally trouble-free, but you have every right to expect material purchased from this store to be in perfect condition when you buy it. We sincerely appreciate your bringing this matter to our attention.

We make every effort to see that each piece of equipment we sell is thoroughly inspected before it leaves the store. Unfortunately, through an oversight of one of our employees, your equipment was not properly inspected.

Our driver is bringing out a fully inspected and warranted Ferranti Hi-Fi Set to replace the one you have. He should be there Wednesday morning by ten o'clock.

Your past patronage during the past four years, Mr. Santoro, is greatly appreciated. We value your friendship as well as your business and we want to make every transaction satisfactory to you and your family. If for any reason it is not, we urge you to bring it to our attention so we can make a proper adjustment.

Please let us know how you like the replacement set you are getting on Wednesday. We would like to know if you like it as well as if you have any trouble.

Sincerely,

Boyd Miller

Customer Service

Much more difficult, of course, is having to tell a customer you can't grant his original claim for adjustment. No one likes to be told, "No, you cant." Nowhere, perhaps, is the element of Preparation more important than in this situation.

The first step toward an effective adjusment letter is a beginning that puts a reader in the right frame of mind. The opening should "get in step" with the reader by emphasizing some point with which he will *agree*.

The original point of contact is also the psychological turning point. The next step is to supply enough factual detail so that the reader will realize the fairness of the decision and agree that it is logical and reasonable. You must make every effort to minimize the complaint and highlight instead your solution. Always try to say YES quickly and gaily, and NO slowly.

The last paragraph of your letter should emphasize service, cooperation, sincere appreciation, or customer satisfaction. It adds a lot of persuasive power to the letter and brings the conciliatory tone to a climax at just the right moment.

Whether you grant a full adjustment, offer a compromise, or make no concession at all, your letter still has a three-fold purpose: to satisfy the reader (1) that he has been treated fairly, (2) to restore his confidence in you, and (3) to regain his goodwill.

The most prevalent reason, it is safe to say, for not granting an adjustment, is the fact that a customer or a client has not done something he was supposed to do. The writer has the problem of pointing this out to the customer withour accusing or otherwise irritating him. Remember, you still want to retain his patronage. Figure 2 is an example of how this was done in a tactful way.

Figure 2

April 21, 19___

Dear Mrs. Monroe:

We are in complete agreement and sympathy with your letter of April 17. Not only do you have a right to rely on an Electromagic Vacuum Cleaner, but it is inconvenient and provoking to have one break down at an inopportune moment. This is why we immediately investigated the problem when you returned your machine.

A complete analysis by our repair department indicates your Electromagic had a burned-out bearing. This malfunction was caused by the machine not having been oiled or cleaned in a long time. Although the Electromagic is guaranteed for one year against all defects in workmanship or materials, we cannot assume responsibility for repairs caused by less than proper care. You understand, of course, we cannot repair your Electromagic free of charge.

However, Mrs. Monroe, we will be more than glad to restore your vacuum cleaner to like-new condition at the actual cost of the parts, or $8.24. When you pick it up, it will be ready to operate. If you will follow the directions for proper maintenance, as given in your instruction booklet, you will get many years of efficient service from your Electromagic Vacuum Cleaner.

Please call our repair department (extension 217) and authorize us to proceed with the repairs. We will call you as soon as it is ready.

Sincerely,

Don Eller

Customer Service

Getting away for a moment from the more or less "average" problems connected with unsatisfactory products or services, we should take a brief look at another difficult area to cope with. This situation occurs when customers insist on taking unjustified discounts on their bills.

Suppose, for example, you or your company had a standard payment policy of "1 ten, net 30" or, in other words, a 1% discount if the bill is paid within 10 days after billing, or total net amount of the bill by the end of 30 days. One of your customers, a Mr. Hollingswood, paid an $847.00 bill almost four weeks late with a check for $838.53. He replied to your second bill for $8.47 by saying, "I don't owe it and I won't pay it!"

Figure 3 is a suggestion for handling this ticklish situation. The amount of the discount is not important, but the principle is, especially if the customer continues to follow a consistent practice of improperly taking the discount.

Figure 3

July 12, 19——

Dear Mr. Hollingswood:

I have just received your letter of July 9 and I do appreciate this opportunity to clear up what I am sure is a misunderstanding.

As you know, for years we have had a standard policy of allowing a one (1) percent discount to customers who pay their bills within ten (10) days of the date of their statement. We have long maintained this policy because we can achieve a comparable saving by paying our bills within ten (10) days. In reality, we are passing these savings on to our customers as a reward for their promptness.

Obviously, we make no savings when our customers do not pay within the ten-day period; therefore, we must adhere to our principle. I think you will agree, Mr. Hollingswood, the $8.47 is, in itself, a trivial matter but, in fairness to everyone, we try to maintain a consistent policy. I also feel you would object, and rightfully so, if you paid the full net amount of your bill within 30 days and someone else, at the same time, was allowed to take a discount after the ten days had expired.

Now that you are in possession of all the facts, I feel quite sure you can understand and appreciate the equity of our policy and the fairness of the $8.47 bill. We want all our customers to take advantage of our discount policy but, at the same time, we want to be fair as well as consistent. I'm sure you agree this is only just and equitable.

Once again, let me thank you for writing to me and giving me the opportunity to clear things up. If I have not cleared them up to your satisfaction, please call me. Only by frank discussion of our problems can we work together for our mutual benefit.

Sincerely,

Doyle Smith

Chief, Accounting Dept.

EFFECTIVELY HANDLING A PARTIAL ADJUSTMENT

There remains, of course, one more category—perhaps the broadest category of all—that of the partial adjustment. One must realize that the refusal to adjust a claim, whether it be partially or completely, must always include a statement that exonerates the company. The claimant must be made to see that he was either partially or wholly responsible. At the same time, however, he can't be made to feel he is being accused or ridiculed in any way or you will surely lose a customer.

Three important points enter into the decision as to whether to wholly refuse a claim or make a partial adjustment. They are:

1. The facts of the case and how well presented;
2. The company's attitude toward unwarranted claims; and
3. The amount of money involved.

In the majority of cases—perhaps 55 to 60% of the time—the amount of the partial adjustment depends on how well a claim is presented. Obviously, if a claim is poorly presented and weakly supported, it will receive little attention indeed. On the contrary, if a claim is well presented and documented, it will at least be checked out in full before a reply is given.

As mentioned earlier, no exact formula will solve all adjustment problems or compose effective letters. However, the letters shown in Figures 4 and 5 are furnished as an example of a good claim and adjustment.

Figure 4

October 2, 19____

Mercury Tire Co, Inc.

Gentlemen:

I purchased a 7.35-14 Mercury tire last March 16 from the Economy Tire and Supply Co., 1201 S. River St. I find it has proved defective after only 6,500 miles. When I took it back to Mr. Samuels at Economy Tire and asked him to replace it for me, he took it but he suggested I write you about it.

Since I have used Mercury Tires for over seven years, I have first hand knowledge about their long mileage and safety.

This kind of past performance makes me curious as to why this particular tire should wear out so rapidly.

In view of the fact I have always had from 22 to 24,000 miles trouble-free use from Mercury Tires, and that I have been caused considerable inconvenience, I feel reasonable certain you will furnish me with a new tire at about a 70% discount, depending on your guarantee.

Very truly yours,

J.C. Trudeau

Figure 5

October 8, 19____

Dear Mr. Trudeau:

We heartily concur with your statement that you should expect more than 6,500 miles of service from the Mercury Tire you wrote us about October 2nd. As you also implied in your letter, Mercury Tires are built to give over 25,000 miles of trouble-free service under normal conditions.

Our Service Department has examined the tire which was sent on to us by Mr. Samuels. Investigation shows your tire was driven when seriously underinflated, which caused the side walls to crack. To clarify this for you even further, we are enclosing a booklet which shows on page 7 a tire damaged in the same manner as yours was.

You will notice we have marked several sections of the booklet with red pencil. If you follow these particular suggestions, you will have no further difficulty of this kind. On the contrary, you will be greatly pleased with the increased mileage you will receive.

We can fully appreciate how you feel about this. Our guarantee of "at least 20,000 miles for Mercury Tires under normal conditions" still holds true. However, your tire, probably without your knowledge, was subjected to a strain which no normal tire could withstand. Therefore, it does not fall technically within the scope of our guarantee.

Nevertheless, since we want to keep you as a satisfied customer and to continue to experience the miles of good service Mercury Tires have long given, we are willing to bear a portion of your loss by offering you a new 7.35-14 Mercury Tire at a thirty percent discount. Just take this letter to Mr. Samuels, or any local dealer, and he will mount your new Mercury Tire for you at the aforementioned price.

We appreciate the opportunity to be of service to you and we trust we can count you as one of our satisfied customers.

Sincerely yours,

James Perkins

Customer Service

Encl

As these letters show, the adjuster has to focus attention on the customer's negligence—that of driving with an underinflated tire. He also had to protect the position of his dealer, Mr. Samuels. This is Mr. Trudeau's only personal contact with the company.

It is better to offer the customer *more* than he asks for if it is practical or convenient; however, it is just as important to do everything possible to make sure the customer not only accepts the proposed adjustment, but is at least satisfied, if not pleased, with the outcome. With the fair and friendly attitude displayed by Mr. Perkins, chances are Mr. Trudeau will accept the settlement offered. Based on the claim he presented, Mr. Trudeau got all he deserved to get. As the chapter title implies, "A claim is what you make it!"

HOW "SPEED MASON" IS APPLIED

This would be an opportune moment to recapitulate the principles covered in the previous chapters pertaining to the five major categories of business letters, i.e., ordinary, sales, credit, collection, and claims. You can readily see that the ten "how" elements of effective communication are equally applicable to all. Let's consider each one:

SOUL

Regardless of which category is involved, the writer must show interest in the reader's (original writer's) problem. In the ordinary letter or sales letter, it inspires confidence, demonstrates sincerity, and shows your desire to be of service and help the reader solve his problem. In credit letters, where you are trying to promote credit business or good will, your interest in the reader will inspire or encourage a positive response. In collection letters, people pay bills mainly due to subjective satisfactions or emotional considerations. Soul includes being patient, understanding the reader's attitude, and working out a solution. In claims letters, it means the writer understands and appreciates the limitations of the reader, and is reasonable enough to consider an equitable adjustment.

PLANNING AND PREPARATION

Sound planning and thoughtful preparation "sets the stage" for putting across your ideas, makes the reader feel important, and creates a favorable impression. In any type of letter, you cannot approach the problem properly without it. It is absolutely necessary if you have to deny a claim, or even offer a reasonable adjustment to a claim. If you are writing a claim, the degree of success you achieve is in direct proportion to the amount of preparation you put into it.

EMOTIONAL STABILITY

In writing any business letter, a calm, tactful, courteous attitude lends strength as well as sincerity to your letter. In either credit or collection letters, if you jump to conclusions because you are being influenced by emotions, you could easily be wrong and be digging a hole too deep from which to extricate yourself. Most important of all, anger, hate, revenge, or any emotion similarly motivated, will never support nor defeat a claim.

EVALUATION

Analysis and evaluation of a writer's problem or proposal is essential to reach the proper decision on which to base your reply. In the case of credit letters, you have to evaluate the credit standing or potential of the prospect in order to determine the approach to use. A writer has to evaluate reactions, or lack of them, to effectively use collection letters. Through evaluation of a claim is part and parcel of the adjustment process, and cannot be done in a haphazard or incomplete manner. In any event, each case is decided on its own merits. This can only be done by a logical and comprehensive evaluation.

DIRECTION

Adequate direction in a business letter systematically resolves the problem, clearly points the way, and restores organization. In a credit environment, the writer uses it to promote either a credit business or cash business. A successful writer must follow certain specific steps in applying the collection letter procedure; therefore, direction is a major factor in the successful accomplishment of your objective–getting payment of the indebtedness. The judicious use of direction is paramount in the orderly disposition of a claim, i.e., what is to be done, and how, when, and where.

MOTIVATION

If anything could be described as a keynote to good business correspondence, it would have to be motivation. A writer usually expects a reader to act in a certain way, so he must be inclined or motivated to act that way. The writer must use vivid, colorful, dramatic words, be enthusiastic and have a convincing close. This is most certainly true in trying to promote a credit business or use of a credit privilege. No one can deny that trying to get a debtor to pay his past due obligations certainly requires motivation of the highest order. Replying to a claim letter requires motivation, whether you are trying to get acceptance of your decision or merely getting concessions pertaining to an adjustment.

ACCEPTABILITY

To gain acceptability on the part of the reader, the writer must give reasons why to support his position. He must also talk in the jargon of the reader to assure adequate comprehension. Promoting credit business certainly involves acceptability of what you have to offer the prospect. On the other hand, if you are *refusing* credit, you should try to make your decision acceptable. Entreaties in all collection letters must be acceptable, otherwise they will be ignored and you will have wasted your time. In order to adequately resolve a claim, the adjustment proposed should be acceptable. Also, a refusal to honor a claim should be acceptable, or else you will lose a customer.

SIMPLICITY

Two of the five "sides" of a good business letter are brevity and simplicity, two closely related characteristics of a writing style leading to a quicker and better understanding. Simplicity promotes and insures a greater understanding of all points, therefore, it helps to promote goodwill. The collection procedure is a difficult one under any condition. Using a simple approach has to help. The same thing can be said of handling claims. Simple language helps to promote acceptance of an adjustment. The reader tends to distrust complex or academic language, feeling the writer is trying to "fast talk" him, shame him, or cover something up.

ORGANIZATION

It almost goes without saying that a writer can't very well map out his plan or his strategy if he is not well organized. In credit and collection letters, the orderly and organized approach is the only way to produce results. In any letter, the message cannot get through to the reader if it is haphazard and disorganized. A reader will not even finish an unorganized or poorly arranged letter.

NOVELTY

The main purpose of the use of novelty is to gain attention of the reader and capture his interest. Therefore, anything you do to gain this objective, without being tricky, is going to help you write a successful letter. It will help you promote business and good will and inspire cooperation. The novel approach in a claim letter helps to make the refusal or the adjustment more palatable. In giving a claimant something less than he asked for in a strictly legal, "school-teacherish," or high-sounding pronouncement is never very appetizing. In fact, it may have the effect of prolonging the issue rather than closing it.

So, you can see, regardless of which type of letter you are trying to write, each one of the ten "how" elements must come into play.

Some, of course, will get more attention than others, but they all should at least be considered. More often than not, one or two have been overlooked. I have seen examples where five or six have been neglected. These letters were a complete waste.

11

Improving the Executive Vocabulary

Do you consider yourself above, below or just about average when it comes to vocabulary? Probably above average, but did you know that the vocabulary of the average adult is only about one-and-one-half times as large as that of a ten year old?

Recent surveys have revealed this astounding fact, but that's not the worst of it! The average person is increasing his vocabulary at only about *one* percent of the rate he was achieving when he was in grammar school!

The average ten year old knows the meanings of approximately 35,000 different words and, since he was six years old, he has been learning new words at a rate of 4 to 5,000 words a year. How do these figures compare with yours?

In today's highly intellectualized society, the man with a better vocabulary stands a much better chance of success in his personal or business life. If you systematically increase your vocabulary, you will improve your facility in handling the English language, build your self-assurance, and also your ability to express your thoughts effectively and efficiently.

The average person, however, finds it too difficult or, at least, a dull routine to conscientiously and regularly build up his vocabulary.

We would agree, of course, if he is merely going to sit down to read cultural literature and flush out new and different words for his vocabulary cache everyday, it would be dull indeed. This is why we don't recommend using such an approach.

If you're really serious about increasing your vocabulary, you will have to make vocabulary building a hobby, an absorbing interest, perhaps even an obsession, as it was with many well known authors. You will surely benefit from it.

One of the foremost things a person must do to make effective strides in the direction of increasing his storehouse of words, is to retain or recapture his "human urge to learn" with which he was born. If you can do this, you can keep increasing your vocabulary at an amazing rate—*no matter how old you are!*

TEN STEPS TO A BETTER VOCABULARY

If you do have this "human urge to learn," and want to both intellectually expand your horizons and build a better vocabulary, here are ten valuable suggestions for you to follow:

1. You will have to read more. This you can't avoid. You will find most of the sources of your supply of new words in newspapers, books, and magazines. If you don't read them, you don't increase your vocabulary—it's as simple as that. It's like pouring oil in the crankcase—you have to use a funnel.

2. You must become acutely aware of and receptive to new words. Words won't come looking for you—you must constantly be on the lookout for words you haven't heard or seen before.

3. You are obliged to learn to add to your own vocabulary the new words you *meet* in your reading. When you see a new word, don't just go on reading—pause for a moment—think about it—get used to its sound and appearance. Try to figure out its meaning from the context of the sentence. What has happened is, by this process, you have become highly *conscious* of the word and you will notice it more frequently in the future.

   You now have a special awareness of it. Before long, you will know what it rightfully means and you will find it easy to use on your own. If you want, when you encounter an unusual word, go to a good dictionary. It is not essential, however, to thumb through the dictionary for every new word you find.

4. You must open your mind to new ideas. As said before, when your vocabulary stops growing, your mind stops growing. For instance, think of a subject you may be interested in. Choose several books and pamphlets on it to read. You will soon be well schooled on that

subject, at least from a layman's point of view. You will find, the more you do this, the more enjoyable it will become and the more of it you will want to do.

5. Master facts and words you need to know. You, of course, should try to funnel your efforts in the particular science, technology, or field of interest you are working in, in order to put across your ideas or express yourself as you should.

6. Pay close attention to well informed people. These types are the ones who have the knowledge and, therefore, the familiarity with the words related to that knowledge.

7. Get in the habit of using *exact* and expressive words, rather than vague, general, and "heavy" words. One of the biggest stumbling blocks people have is the lack of ability to express themselves *as they want or should.* Learn the exact and organic meaning of words and try to use them to fit the case whenever you can. It's just as easy to learn as any other system.

8. Observe the ways of words in actual use. You will learn a lot of things by watching and listening to how words are "put together" to express a certain idea or intent. Profit by the experience or expertise of others.

9. Study the formation and origin of words or, as I like to call it, the "family trees of words." This concept is explained in further detail in this chapter.

10. Last, but not least, you must *set a goal.* By determined, conscious effort you can learn several hundred, maybe even several thousand new words in the next year. Set yourself a goal of five or six new words each day. This may sound too ambitious, but you will soon find, when you start *actively* searching for new words in your reading exploits, those new words are all around you.

Learning new words is a lot easier than you may think—provided you go about it the right way. The secret of successful vocabulary building is *repetition.* To add a new word to your vocabulary and not lose it, you must understand its origin, see or hear it in several different contexts and in a variety of forms.

HOW TO USE THE "FAMILY TREES OF WORDS"

To enable you to develop a facility for learning new words and understanding how they work in actual practice, I will outline the concept of vocabulary building I mentioned earlier, which I call the "Family Trees of Words."

It is not the only system, or even necessarily the best one, but I have found it easy to learn and very effective in teaching and encouraging others to build their own vocabulary in a fairly rapid fashion.

Vocabulary building may be compared to a house. The root is the foundation, giving it body, size, and strength; the prefix is the roof and siding, providing it with style and character; and the suffix is the landscaping, for supplying the finishing touch. You can change them all around, adding any variations you want to get any kind of house, with any kind of structure, coloring, or outward appearance.

What so many people do not realize is that a word can be taken apart just as if it were a mechanical gadget. Perhaps you have never thought of a word in this way before. But when you do, it changes your entire approach to vocabulary building. It will make it far easier for you. Suddenly the mystique of where words come from, the difficult and onerous task of memorizing them, the bother of having to look them up, vanishes. Most words in our language have three parts:

1. Prefix—beginning (direction of meaning)

2. Root, base, stem, or "chassis"—(middle, main meaning)

3. Suffix—ending (shade of meaning)

Getting at the roots of words—taking words apart—is one of the most effective ways of fixing the meanings of words. By looking at all three (prefix-root-suffix), we are going to discover what makes a word tick and how we can remember it.

We advocate this method, however, only *after* you know the meaning of the word. If you do it beforehand, you can go up the garden path or, that is, arrive at the wrong answer.

Vocabulary is a forest of word trees and these trees, in many cases, are related to each other or have a common origin—in other words, they may be called "family trees." Roots are the *surnames* for a family tree of words. When you learn one root and what it means you have, in effect, learned about 20 other words that relate to it. To clarify this point, here are some examples:

1.The root (word sign) for the word *make* is FAC. FAC comes from the Latin verb *facere,* meaning *to do* or *make.* Look at the family of words that "fall out" of the FAC tree:

fact	satisfaction	faction
factory	facile	factitious
factious	facility	factive
factor	facilitate	facticide

| faculty | facient | facsimile |
| putrefaction | dissatisfaction | manufacture |

2. Does that strike you as odd? Not at all. Let's take a look at another one. The root for the word *draw* or *pull* is TRACT. TRACT comes from the Latin verb *tractare*, meaning *to draw out*. Here are some of the word "nuts" we find in the TRACT tree:

tractile	extract	attract
intractable	detract	attractive
traction	protract	abstract
tractor	protracted	distract
contract	tractable	subtract
contraction	tractability	retract

3. Just to prove our point, let's try one more—the JEC tree, which is the root word for *throw* or *lie*. JEC stems from the Latin verb *jacere*, meaning *to throw:*

conject	dejection	eject
conjecture	inject	injection
deject	object	projection
ejection	objection	rejection
interjection	adjective	abject

Vocabulary building, however, is more than just learning new words. Being able to translate formal and technical language into everyday language with meaning you are sure of is an important verbal skill. It is especially important in higher education, where such a vocabulary is in common use. Skill in handling words, therefore, becomes a requirement for success.

Skill in handling words means that you can master academic language. You are not overwhelmed by the "big words," but rather have sufficient confidence through knowledge of how words operate to be able to recognize and utilize the academic style. You will find it necessary to become familiar with Latin and Greek derivatives, because the vocabulary of the academic world is based, in the main, on word elements from these languages.

You may not recognize them for what they are, but it has been said that English is 50% Latin, 25% Greek, 15% German, and 10% of all others. So, you see, if you are familiar with most of the Latin and Greek roots, you have a good grasp of about 75% of the English language or, if you like, "American English."

TRANSLATING LITERAL MEANINGS

Vocabulary is generally built by combinations of word elements, or parts, called prefix, root, and suffix. For example, in the word "deportment," DE is the prefix, PORT is the root, and MENT is, of course, the suffix. Sometimes, though, a prefix and a root element put together are hard to pronounce, such as "in-possible" (not possible). It is therefore made easier to pronounce by calling it IMpossible. This process is called *assimilation,* and is why all forms of the prefixes or roots do not always retain their *exact* spelling when they are put together to form a word.

One more skill in addition to recognizing variations in spelling is needed. That is the use of literal meanings to help us arrive at a modern meaning. For example:

"Although George Bernard Shaw asserted that he was not hard to contact, the facts known about him proved he was a person who was not easy to get to."

The word "inaccessible" would be substituted for the last nine words in the above (a person who was not easy to get to) and would sound better by so doing. The strictly literal translation of "inaccessible" (in the order of word elements) is "NOT-TO-GO-ABLE-TO." These are the meanings associated with IN, AC, CESS and IBLE. You have to be able to fit these literal meanings into the context, to the way the word is used.

Despite difficulties such as these, which are certainly not as cumbersome as they might seem, there are many compensations. Knowledge of derivation allows us to:

1. Help fix the meaning of words which, obviously, is the most important facet of all.
2. Frequently wind up with many other associated words to add to our vocabulary.
3. Get insights into familiar words, e.g., *discredit* means "take away (dis) belief (cred) in or from (it)."
4. Learn how rewarding an experience it can be to use a good dictionary.

If all you know about a word is its superficial meaning, you do not really know the word. If you meet someone interesting, you want to know more about him—where he comes from, his line of work, his other interests, etc. It's the same with words. If you know where a word comes from and what it does in a sentence, then you are intimately familiar with the word and you are qualified to use it effectively in the future.

One more point—practice *pronouncing* and *spelling* each new word. It isn't *your* word until you can say and spell it right. Other people will easily notice your mistake if you do it wrong.

THREE WORD LISTS

Figures 1, 2, and 3 which follow comprise word and word-sign lists for you to work with. Figure 1 is a list of Prefixes, Figure 2 a list of Suffixes, and Figure 3 a list of Root-Sign Words.

These lists are based on common, everyday words most frequently used and known, not on scientific or technical jargon or other branches of language. I strongly recommend you quickly scan each list to become familiar with the *total* concept before concentrating on any particular list. Each list has its own purpose, and yet they all work together.

Most all indices of prefixes, roots, and suffixes (vocabulary) are listed by the prefix, suffix, or the strange looking root name. These lists, however, are arranged alphabetically by the *English* meaning for ease in finding and using the correct word elements. For example, the root for *bend* is FLEC or FLEX and will be found under the word *bend.* One or more example words are given on each list for each word-sign.

Some symbols, even though shown as Roots, are usually used as Prefixes, e.g., MICRO (small), PED (foot), THEO (God).

A word should be said about Suffixes. Even though they play only a minor role in influencing the meaning of a word, they also serve as tags to identify the word as a noun, verb, adjective or adverb.

An interesting and challenging game to play is to take a Root-Sign and see how many different words you can find using that particular root. Try it out on your friends.

To use these lists more efficiently, you should *analyze* and *synthesize* words from time to time; that is, tear a word apart and then put it back together again. Here are some examples:

No. 1: English meaning: Alive (First word-sign on list, Figure 3)
        Root-Sign(s): VIT and VIV

Examples:	VITalize	—give life to
	VIVacity	—having vital force
Word to Analyze: Vivisection		VIVI —Root —alive
		SECT—Root —cut (cutting)
		TION—Suffix—act of

Synthesize to: Act of cutting alive

Other words: VITal   —Relating to life
                 VITals   —Vital organs
                 VITamin   —Essential food element
                 VITascope   —Motion picture projector
                 VIVacious   —Full of life
                 VIVarium   —Small glass hot house for plants
                 reVIVe   —Bring back to life
                 surVIVe   —Live through an ordeal

No. 2: English meaning: Answer (Third word-sign on Root List)
        Root-Sign: SPON

Examples: reSPONse   —reply to
              reSPONsible   —answerable

Word to analyze: irreSPONsible IR   —Prefix—not
                                RE   —Prefix—back, to
                                SPONS—Root —answer
                                IBLE   —Suffix—able to

Synthesize to: Not able (unable) to answer to

Other words: reSPONsibility —Reliability
                 reSPONdent   —One who replies
                 unreSPONsive   —Not answering
                 correSPONd   —To cummunicate
                 reSPONsive   —Answering in kind
                 reSPONd   —To answer
                 SPONsor   —One who assumes responsibility
                 SPONsorship   —State of being a sponsor

Figure 1

List of Prefixes

Meaning	Prefix	Example	Definition
Above, Over	EPI	EPIgraph	Opening quotation
	HYPER	HYPERtension	Excessive tension
	OVER	OVERlay	Spread over
	SUPER	SUPERior	Higher rank
	SUR	SURveillance	Watching over
Absence of	AN	ANemic	Deficient in red blood cells
		ANonymous	Without a name
Across	TRA	TRAverse	Span across
	TRANS	TRANSport	Carry across
After	POST	POSTmortem	After death
		POSTscript	Written afterward
Again	RE	REstate	State again
		REvise	Do over
Against	ANTI	ANTIpathy	Feeling of dislike
	CONTRA	CONTRAvene	Oppose in argument
	OB	OBdurate	Persistent wrongdoing
All	PAN	PANacea	Cure all
		PANchromatic	Having all colors
Alone, Sole	MONO	MONOlogue	One person discourse
		MONOpoly	Rule by one
Apart (from)	DIS	DISparity	Difference between

Meaning	Prefix	Word	Definition
	SE	SEquester	Set apart
Around, About	AMBI	AMBIent	Moving around
	CIRCUM	CIRCUMnavigate	Sail around
	PERI	PERImeter	Boundary of a closed figure
Away	AB	ABort	Cut short
	ABS	ABStain	Hold off from
	APO	APOgee	Farthest point in orbit
	SE	SEcrete	Hide away
Back	RE	REcoil	Wind back
	RETRO	RETROactive	Extend back to prior time
Bad	MAL	MALevolent	Wishing evil
	MIS	MIScreant	Evil doer
Before	ANTE	ANTEcedent	Word preceding
	PRE	PREscient	Knowing beforehand
Behind	POST	POSTerior	Rear end or later
	POST	POSTilion	One who rides as a guide
Below	SUB	SUBordinate	Lower in rank
	UNDER	UNDERcover	Hidden in meaning or fact
Beside	PARA	PARAgraph	Section of a composition
	PARA	PARAllel	Evenly side by side
Between	INTER	INTERcept	Take before delivery
	INTER	INTERvene	Come between
Beyond	EXTRA	EXTRAsensory	Beyond ordinary senses
	OUT	OUTlast	Last longer
	TRANS	TRANScendent	Of a higher level
	ULTRA	ULTRAmodern	Beyond modern usage
Both	AMBI	AMBIdextrous	Use both hands

Meaning	Prefix	Example	Definition
	AMPHI	AMPHIbious	Both water and land
		AMPHIlogism	Double talk
Deprive	DIS	DISable	Deprive of use
		DISinherit	Deprive of inheritance
Down	CATA	CATAract	Large waterfall
	DE	DEbark	Get off a ship
Eight	OCT	OCTagonal	Eight sided
Every	PAN	PANdemic	Relating to all people
		PANorama	Whole picture shown in parts
Excessive	HYPER	HYPERbole	Exaggeration; figure of speech
	MACRO	MACROlogy	Lot of talking
	ULTRA	ULTRAsonic	Beyond sound
External	OUT	OUTside	Outer side of a boundary
		OUTward	Moving toward outside
Facing	OB	OBjective	Goal or target (being faced)
		OBlong	Rectangle longer than wide
False	PSEUDO	PSEUDOnym	False name
Five	PENTA	PENTAgon	Five sided
	QUIN	QUINtuplet	One of five children
For, Forth, Forward	PRO	PROmise	To warrant or assure
		PROvide	Supply what is needed
Four	QUAD	QUADrangle	Four-sided figure
	QUAT	QUATrain	Four lines of a verse
	TETRA	TETRAmeter	Verse of four feet
From	AB	ABsolve	Free from blame
	APO	APOlogy	Attempt to make amends

Meaning	Prefix	Example	Definition
Good	DE	DEtract	Take away
	BENE	BENEficial	Good and wholesome
	BON	BONus	Reward
	EU	EUphony	Pleasant sound
Half	DEMI	DEMItasse	Very small cup
	HEMI	HEMIsphere	Half a globe
	SEMI	SEMIsweet	Half sweet
In, Into	EM	EMbrace	Take into one's arms
	EN	ENroll	Sign in
	IN	INdulge	Take pleasure in
	INTRO	INTROvert	Looking inwardly
Intensive-ness (quality)	BE	BEloved	Loved with great intensity
	BE	BErate	Scold harshly
Large	MACRO	MACROcosm	The universe
	MACRO	MACROdont	Having large teeth
Many, Much	MULTI	MULTIple	Group of many
	POLY	POLYgamy	Many marriages
Nine	NOV	NOVena	Nine days
Not	A	Anachronism	Error in chronology
	IL	ILlogical	Not logical
	IN	INconclusive	Not conclusive
	IR	IRrational	Not rational
	NON	NONcommittal	Unclear attitude
	UN	UNnatural	Not natural
On	IN	INscribe	Write upon
	IN	INvoke	Call upon
One, Once	MONO	MONOtony	One tone or sound

Opposed,	UNI	UNIverse	One body of things
Opposite	ANTI	ANTIbody	Body opposed to another
Out	CONTRA	CONTRAband	Illegal traffic
	E	Elaborate	Build up or out
	EC	EClipse	Cut out light
	EF	EFfusive	Excessively demonstrative
	EX	EXtract	Take out
Outside	EXTRA	EXTRAdite	Hand over to authority
		EXTRApolate	Project or extend
Power	DYN	DYNamite	Explosive
		DYNamo	Forceful generator
Resemble	PARA	PARAble	Story showing comparison
		PARAdise	Like heaven
Reverse	UN	UNconcerned	Not concerned
Separate	DIS	DISengage	Release or detach
		DISlocate	Put out of place
Seven	SEPT	SEPTennial	Seventh year
Six	HEX	HEXagonal	Six sided
	SEX	SEXtet	Group of six
Take away	DIS	DISarm	Remove arms
		DIScourage	Deprive of courage
Ten	DEC	DECimate	Cut into tenths
Thoroughly	PER	PERsecute	Thoroughly harass
		PERvade	Diffuse throughout
Three, Thrice	TRI	TRIplex	Three-unit building
Through	DIA	DIAlogue	Conversation thru 2 or more
	PER	PERmeate	Penetrate through

Meaning	Prefix	Example	Definition
To, Toward	AD	ADvance	Move toward
		ADvice	Speak to
Together	COM	COMpact	Place together
	CON	CONtrive	Plan together
	SYL	SYLlable	Two Vowels with one sound
	SYM	SYMphony	Consonance of sounds
	SYN	SYNchronize	Arrange events to coincide
	SYS	SYStem	Interacting or interdependent group of items
Two, twice	BI	BIcycle	Two-wheeled vehicle
	DI	DImerous	Consists of two parts
	DU	DUalize	To make dual
Upon	EPI	EPIdermis	Layer of skin on body
		EPItaph	Inscription on gravestone
Within	INTRA	INTRAcontinental	Within the continent
		INTRAmural	Within the student body
Withdraw, Without	SE	SEcede	Withdraw
		SEgregate	Set apart
Wrong	MIS	MISdeed	Wrongful act
		MIStake	Error

Figure 2

List of Suffixes

Meaning	Suffix	Example
Able to	ABLE	Tenable
	BLE	Soluble
	IBLE	Edible
Action	AGE	Badinage
	ANCE	Remonstrance
	ANCY	Relevancy
	ATION	Adulation
	ING	Dancing
	ION	Function
	MENT	Estrangement
Act upon	ATE	Liberate
Being	ATE	Emanate
	ID	Placid
Belief	ISM	Socialism
Belong- ing to	ORY	Memory
Cause to	ATE	Consolidate
	EN	Lengthen
Charac- teristic	ISH	Amateurish
	SOME	Lithesome
	Y	Fatty
Collection	AGE	Salvage
Come to be	EN	Blacken
Connected with	ORY	Respiratory
Expert	IAN	Librarian
Full of	FUL	Resourceful
	OSE	Bellicose
	OUS	Vitreous
	ULENT	Corpulent
Having	ATE	Sensate
	EN	Frozen
In the manner of	LY	Succinctly
Like	AL	Autumnal
	ANT	Verdant
	EN	Wooden

Meaning	Suffix	Example
	IC	Angelic
	ICAL	Spherical
	ILE	Infantile
	INE	Leonine
	LIKE	Lifelike
	LY	Regally
	OID	Asteroid
Make	IFY	Petrify
	ISE	Chastise
	IZE	Publicize
Native of	AN	African
	IAN	Mongolian
Of, Related to	AC	Cardiac
	ACIOUS	Tenacious
	AL	Radical
	ANT	Ascendant
	AR	Stellar
	ERN	Northern
	IC	Archaic
	ICAL	Biographical
	INE	Serpentine
	LIKE	Ghostlike
Office	ATE	Potentate
One who (is	ANT	Appellant
or does)	AR	Beggar
	ARD	Slaggard
	ATE	Surrogate
	EER	Engineer
	ENT	President
	ER	Planner
	IER	Flier
	IST	Modernist
	OR	Actor
	EE	Devotee
	ITE	Suburbanite
Of - (Be-	AN	European
long to)	ARY	Documentary
	IAN	Reptilian
	ORY	History
Performing	IVE	Aggressive
Place of	AGE	Storage
Place where	ARIUM	Planetarium

	ARY	Library
	ERY	Bakery
	ORY	Crematory
Process	ATION	Purification
	ING	Printing
	ION	Extension
Resembling	OID	Anthropoid
Small	ETTE	Kitchenette
	LET	Droplet
	LING	Duckling
	ULE	Capsule
State of	ANCE	Abundance
	ANCY	Militancy
	CY	Regency
	DOM	Boredom
	ENCE	Competence
	HOOD	Manhood
	ION	Suspension
	ISM	Despotism
	ITY	Quality
	MENT	Contentment
	MONY	Matrimony
	NESS	Dullness
	OR	Behavior
	SHIP	Fellowship
	TUDE	Lassitude
	Y	Equality
Tending		
toward	IVE	Restive
That	ER	Wrecker
which	ICE	Service
	IVE	Active
	MONY	Testimony
	OR	Tractor
	URE	Rapture
Without	LESS	Penniless

Figure 3

List of Roots

Meaning	Root	Example (Definition)
Alive	VIT	VITalize (give life to)
	VIV	VIVacity (having vital force)
All	OMNI	OMNIbus (Providing for many things)
	PAN	PANdemic (Relating to all people)
Answer	SPON	reSPONse (reply); reSPONsible (answerable)
Ask	ROG	interROGate (question)
Bear witness	TEST	atTEST (certify, affirm); TESTify (bear witness)
Begin	ARCH	hierARCH (church leader)
	NASC	reNASCence (rebirth)
	NAT	NATuralize (give citizenship)
Believe	CRED	CREDulous (inclined to believe)
Bend	FLEC	genuFLECt (bend the knee)
	FLEX	FLEXile (tractable nature)
Birth	GEN	GENeric (belonging to race)
	NAT	NATional (relating to a nation)
Bitter	ACER	ACERbity (bitterness)
	ACID	ACIDemia (overacid condition)
	ACRI	ACRImonious (quarrelsome)
Body	CORP	CORPoreal (having a material body)
Break	RUPT	corRUPT (morally depraved (breaking moral law)
Breath	ANIM	ANIMated (having life)
	SPIR	inSPIRed (infused with spirit)

Bring	FER	preFERence (selection); transFER (convey)
Build	STRU	conSTRUction (building); inSTRUctor (teacher)
Call	VOC	VOCation (call to serve)
	VOK	proVOKe (call forth anger)
Carry	FER	conFERence (bringing together)
	GEST	GESTure (use of motion to carry attention)
	PORT	imPORT (carry goods or meaning)
Cause caus	CAUS	beCAUSe (for that reason)
cus	CUS	exCUSe (reason for)
Change,	VERS	obVERSe (face opposite)
turn	VERT	inVERT (turn upside down)
	VIC	VICarious (substitute)
Circle	CYCL	CYCLometer (instrument used to measure circles)
Citizen	CIVI	CIVIlization (cultural development of man)
Claim	CLAIM	proCLAIM (declare openly)
	CLAM	exCLAMatory (spoken in loud manner)
Close	CLUD	ocCLUDe (shut the way)
	CLUS	inCLUSion (act of taking or closing in)
Clothe	VEST	inVEST (clothe with authority); traVESTy (disguise to make a thing ridiculous)
Come	VEN	eVENtual (final coming); interVENtion (between)
Conquer	VANQ	VANQuish (overcome; subdue)
	VICT	conVICT (prove guilty; conquer doubt)
	VINC	inVINCible (unable to be beaten)
Cut	CIS	preCISion (cutting exactly)
	SECT	interSECT (cut between)
Death	MOR	imMORtal (not subject to death)

Degree	GRAD	GRADual (proceed by degree); GRADuate (promote)
Direct	RECT	RECTitude (uprightness)
	REG	REGulate (govern according to rule)
Distant	TELE	TELEpathy (distant communication)
Do	AG	AGile (move quickly)
	FAC	putreFACtion (causing decay)
	FIC	proFICient (able to do things well)
Draw	TRACT	conTRACT (draw together); proTRACT (draw further
Empty	VAC	eVACuate (remove); VACation (rest from work)
End	FIN	deFINite (having limits); reFINe (purify)
Enough	SAT	SATiate (satisfy fully); SATisfactory (giving enough of what is wanted)
Equal	EQU	consEQUence (result equal to cause)
Faith	FEAL	FEALty (devotion to duty)
	FEDER	conFEDERate (united for a purpose)
	FID	conFIDence (self reliance; faith in self)
Father	PATER	PATERnity (fatherhood)
	PATR	PATRicide (murder of one's father)
	PATH	PATHos (feeling of compassion)
Feel,	PASS	imPASSioned (intense feeling)
Feeling	SENS	SENSuous (Preoccupied with feelings)
	SENT	conSENT (feel agreement with)
Fire	VOLCAN	VOLCANic (like a volcano)
First	VULCAN	VULCANian (relating to iron work)
	PRIM	PRIMer (first book); PRIMordial (fundamental
Flow	FLU	conFLUence (flowing together of streams)
Fold	PLIC	imPLICate (fold or twist together)
Follow	PLEX	comPLEX (two or more parts folded together)

Foot	PED	PEDestal (base of statue)
	POD	PODiatry (branch of medicine dealing with feet)
Force	PEL	comPEL (drive or urge)
	PUL	imPULSE (inclination to drive)
Free	LIBER	LIBERtine (person without morals)
Friendly	LIVER	deLIVERy (freedom from; transport to)
	AMIC	AMICable (characterized by good will); AMICus curiae (friend of the court)
Give	TRIB	atTRIBute (give as cause); disTRIBute (give to)
Go	CED	interCEDe (go between)
	CESS	proCESSion (going forward)
	GRAD	deGRADe (go down in fact or judgment)
	GRESS	eGRESS (a way out)
Great	MAGN	MAGNanimous (generous to a fault)
	MEGA	MEGAphone (device to magnify sound)
Group	GREG	GREGarious (moving with group); conGREGate (group together)
Hand	MAN	MANifest (apparent; at hand); MANipulate (manage by hand)
Hang	PEND	PENDulous (hanging down)
	PENS	susPENSe (hanging in air)
Head	CAPI	CAPItate (form a head)
	CAPT	CAPTion (heading)
Health	SAL	SALubrious (favorable to well being)
Hear	AUD	AUDience (group of listeners); AUDible (heard)
Heart	CORD	CORDial (from the heart)
Heavy	COUR	COURage (mental or moral strength)
	GRAV	agGRAVate (increase; make heavier); GRAVitate (obey law of gravity)

Hold	TAIN	conTAIN (keep within limits)
	TEN	mainTENance (act of keeping up)
	TINU	conTINUE (hold or maintain pace)
Hundred	CENT	CENTenary (one hundred)
Inform	NOUNC	deNOUNCe (inform against)
	NUNC	eNUNCiate (pronounce (inform) carefully)
Join	JUNCT	conJUNCTion (word that joins two others)
Judge	JUDIC	JUDICial (relating to a judgement)
Kill	CID	matriCIDe (killing of one's mother)
Kind	GEN	GENeric (relating to all kinds); indiGENous (inborn; innate)
Know	GNI	recoGNIze (see something previouly known)
	GNOS	proGNOSis (prospects for recovery)
	NOT	NOTion (theory of knowledge)
Last	ULTIMA	ULTIMAte (final); ULTIMAtum (last offer)
Laugh (ter)	RID	RIDiculous (laughable)
	RISI	deRISIvely (mockingly)
Law	JUR	conJURe (swear together)
	JUS	adJUStment (amicable legal settlement)
	LEG	LEGitimate (according to law)
Lead	DUC	eDUCate (teach; lead out of ignorance); traDUCe (slander; lead erroneous charge)
Letter:	LITER	LITERature (composition of letters)
Life,	BIO	BIOgraphy (story of life)
Alive	VIT	VITality (state of being alive)
Light	LUC	eLUCidate (bring into light)
	LUMIN	LUMINous (full of light)

Like	SIMIL	SIMILitude (resemblance)
	SIMUL	SIMULant (one who acts like someone else)
Limit	FIN	FINale (conclusion); FINial (end of gutter)
Live	HAB	HABitat (natural living quarters);
		reHABilitate (remake to live again)
Loving	PHIL	PHILanthropist (lover of mankind);
		PHILatelist (stamp collector; lover of)
Man	ANTHRO	ANTHROpology (study of man)
	HUM	HUMility (meekness of man)
Mark	SIGN	deSIGNated (selected; marked)
Marriage	GAM	monoGAMy (one marriage)
Measure	METER	diaMETER (distance across a circle)
	METR	METRical (relating to measurement)
Memory	MEM	MEMorable (worth remembering)
Middle	MEDI	MEDIation (intervention): MEDIocrity (in
		the middle as far as quality is concerned)
More	PLU	PLUrality (state of being numerous)
Move	AG	AGitate (stir up)
	CED	interCEDe (move between)
	CESS	proCESS (going forward)
	MO	MOtivate (cause to move or act)
Name	NOMIN	NOMINal (in name only); NOMINee (one named)
New	NEO	NEOlogy (use of new words)
	NOV	NOVelty (newness)
Order	ORD	inORDinate (out of order)
Other	ALI	ALIen (not a citizen)
	ALLO	ALLOnym (name of another)
	ALTER	ALTERcation (dispute with another)

Paint	HETERO	HETEROgeneous (mixture of ingredients)
	PICT	dePICT (portray); PICTorial (rel. to pictures)
Peculiar	IDIO	IDIOsyncrasy (peculiarity); insIDIOus (of a subtle or peculiar origin)
People	DEM	DEMophile (friend of people)
	POPUL	POPULar (relating to people)
	PUBLI	PUBLIcation (published work (dist. to people)
Permit	LIC	ilLICit (illegal); LICense (permit to act)
Place	LOC	disLOCated (out of place)
	POS	POSture (placement of limbs)
Please	POUN	exPOUNd (place before someone)
	GRAT	inGRATiate (worm oneself into favor)
	PLAC	PLACate (soothe feelings)
Point	PUNCT	PUNCTilious (very precise); PUNCtuate (place points in sentences)
Power	POTEN	omniPOTENt (all powerful); POTENtate (ruler)
Roll	VOLU	reVOLUtion (motion around a center)
	VOLV	inVOLVe (enfold or envelop)
Running	DROM	airDROMe (airport); DROMedary (running camel)
Say	DIC	contraDICt (speak against)
See	SCOPE	horoSCOPE (astrologer's chart)
	SPECT	retroSPECT (reflect back upon)
	VID	proVIDent (making provisions for future)
	VIS	enVISion (see in one's mind)
Self	AUTO	AUTOcrat (ruler); AUTOnomy (self government)
Send	MIS	perMISsion (allow to send through)
	MIT	comMIT (entrust or perform; send with)

Show	MONSTR	deMONSTRate (show); reMONSTRate (find fault)
Sleep	DORM	DORMitory (place to sleep)
	HYPN	HYPNotist (one who induces sleep)
Small	MICRO	MICROcosm (small world);
Smoke	FUM	FUMigate (smoke out); FUMish (easily angered)
Sound	PHON	microPHONE (instrument to transmit sound of voice); PHONetics (study of sounds)
Speak	LOC	interLOCutor (one taking part in discussion)
	LOQU	LOQUacious (talkative)
Spirit	ANIM	ANIMation (having life or spirit)
	SPIR	conSPIRe (breathe (plan) together)
Stand	SIST	deSIST (stop; stand still)
	STA	STAndard (one degree to stand on)
	STIT	subSTITute (stand in for)
Star	ASTER	ASTERisk (tiny star); ASTERoid (like a star)
	ASTRO	ASTROnomy (study of stars)
	STEL	STELlar (relating to a star)
Stick	HER	adHERe (stick to)
	HES	coHESion (sticking together)
Straight	RECT	RECTify (make right); diRECTion (going straight)
Strength	VAL	equiVALent (equal strength); VALidity (legality)
Strong	FORC	enFORCe (give force to)
	FORT	FORTify (make strong)
Stretch	TEND	preTEND (make-believe (stretch a point)
	TENS	inTENSify (make more intense)
	TENT	atTENTion (concentrate; stretch the mind)
Surrender	CEDE	conCEDE (yield to)

Take	CESS	reCESSion (going back to a lower point)
	CAP	CAPtivate (seize)
	CEP	deCEPtion (taking by fraud)
	SUM	asSUMe (take or suppose); conSUMer (user)
	PUT	PUTation (act of thinking); rePUTation (public opinion or thinking)
Think		
Throw	JECT	eJECTion (throwing out); reJECT (throw back)
	PEL	rePEL (throw back); imPEL (throw into)
	PULS	exPULSion (being thrown out)
Time	CHRON	CHRONicle (record of events)
	TEMPOR	conTEMPORary (living at same time)
Touch	TACT	TACTful (having tact)
	TAG	conTAGious (catching through touch)
	TANG	TANGent (touching line)
	TING	conTINGent (depending on future event)
True	VER	VERifiable (can be verified)
Twist	TORS	TORSion (turning in opposite directions)
	TORT	exTORTion (taking by force; illegally)
Vital	GERM	GERManity (relationship; kinship)
Walk	AMB	perAMBulate (travel around)
	GRESS	diGRESS (step aside)
Water	MIGR	eMIGRant (one leaving a country)
	HYDR	HYDRotherapy (water treatment)
	MAR	MARiner (sailor)
	MER	MERmaid (marine creature)
Wisdom	SOPH	SOPHisticated (worldly-wise)
Word	LOG	LOGomania (mania for talking)

Work	OPER	coOPERate (work in unison)
	OPUS	OPUSculum (a minor work)
Write	GRAPH	lithoGRAPHy (reproducing writing)
	SCRIB	subSCRIBe (underwrite or support)
	SCRIP	inSCRIPtion (words engraved on)
Year	ANNU	ANNUity (amount paid annually)
	ENNI	centENNIal (occurring once every 100 years)
Yield	CEDE	acCEDE (go along with)
	FER	coniFERous (cone bearing)

12

How to Avoid Misused
Words and Find
Better Ones

Mark Twain once said, "The difference between the right word and the "almost right" word is the difference between lightning and the lightning bug."

You no doubt have seen this disparity demonstrated many, many times and wondered why the writer—perhaps even you—had not taken the time or pains to use the correct word. More than likely the writer *assumed* he used the right word and later found out, to his embarrassment, he was wrong.

Even more unfortunate is the fact that he may never have *realized* the word or words were wrong and someone else noticed it. The impression the writer created was, in a sense, damaging but he was totally unaware of his mistake.

Words, being symbols of the language, are best used with accuracy. Their purpose is to convey explicit information, which is supposed to be helpful in making or clarifying a point for the reader. If they fail to do this, they make it harder for the reader to understand what the writer wants to say, or they may completely mislead the reader. The latter may have grave consequences.

RULES TO HELP YOU

In order not to mislead your reader, or make it unnecessarily difficult for him to follow you, you should always try to choose the right words as much as you can. To help you to this end, here are four suggested rules to follow:

1. *Depend on short, simple words.* For three big reasons, these types of words are more useful to businessmen than long, complicated words. They are:

    a. The common word is more likely to be understood.

    b. Such words consume less time for all concerned.

    c. They call less attention to writing style.

Examples: Use *about* instead of approximately; *aware* instead of cognizant; *change* instead of modification or alteration; *use* instead of employ or utilize.

2. *Practice using sincere words.* People don't usually trust those who are or appear to be insincere. Our sincerity is usually open to question when we use:

    a. Superlatives without proof;

    b. Surprise, unless it is really beneficial;

    c. Too many adjectives and adverbs;

    d. Euphemisms (better sounding words);

    e. Statements that are not original; or

    f. Careless or unfounded predictions.

3. *Use words economically.* If you have the proper consideration for your reader, you will try to save him time. One way to do this is to be concise. Use just enough words to adequately convey the meaning you intend. Avoid using redundancies and other unnecessary words. Since the meanings of the following words are similar to each other, one of them is unnecessary and should be eliminated (usually in the editing process):

Refer back to	Each and every
True facts	Exact same
Whether or not	Exactly identical
Personal opinion	Basic fundamentals
Full and complete	Concensus of opinion

4. *Strive to give a clear picture.* How well we succeed in painting the right mental picture is determined mainly by the words we choose. Words are merely tools in the process. Like an artist, the writer chooses certain tools or words to make his picture clear. The most reliable words for this purpose are (i) the concrete, specific noun and (ii) the action verb. Examples:

Original	*Revised*
Analysis of the proposal indicates that Mr. Mackey is right	I think Mr. Mackey is right
Termination of your facilities lease is effective on June 30	Your facilities lease expires June 30

Experience has shown us, aside from trying to build a better vocabulary, there are two significant areas (perhaps three) which warrant special attention if a person wants to be able to express himself well. If he can do this, he will write a more effective letter or report, and he will create a more favorable impression.

His image will be improved with his superiors as well as other readers, be they his peers, prospects, customers, or employees.

USE OF "VOGUE" WORDS

The two most important areas cover (i) common misused words and (ii) overused words. The third area, which is of only slightly less concern, involves the use of so-called popular, modern, or "vogue" words. Use of these words may not be any more accurate or correct than other synonyms we could use, but they have become accepted as "in" words and the speaker or author may receive a certain amount of additional respect because he used them.

People in high places or in the public eye today are concerned with their "image." They no longer engage in debates or attend conferences, they take part in "dialogues." These catchy words are called "vogue" words by many authorities. Figure 1 is a list of about 25 of them for your information and use.

Figure 1

Popular Vogue Words

Accolade	—crowning praise
Ambience	—pervading atmosphere

Bellwether	—leader in a particular endeavour
Cachet	—seal of approval
Charisma	—someone in the public eye whose personality is especially attractive
Echelon	—another rung of the organizational ladder
Enclave	—an area set apart
Escalate	—carry up to a higher level
Expertise	—special skills and knowledge of a subject
Finalize	—actions to complete a transaction
Guidelines	—blueprints or broad parameters for taking action
Maximize	—improve something to a high degree or assign maximum importance
Minimize	—reduce costs or problems to a minimum
Mystique	—mystical qualities or attitude about a place or thing
Negotiate	—give and take to resolve an issue
Optimize	—make as perfect as possible
Ploy	—synonym for device or maneuver
Posture	—collection of opinions one has of a subject
Proliferates	—spreads like wildfire
Serendipity	—discovery made while looking for something else
Spectrum	—whole range or scope of activity
Syndrome	—combination of symptoms
Target	—goal or goals management is shooting for
Trauma	—scarring or emotional experience
Viable	—economy, industry or business that is expected to survive

HOW TO AVOID CERTAIN MISUSED WORDS

A listing of the 60 most commonly misused words is given in Figure 2. The two words (in each case) which are used interchangeably and incorrectly are shown side by side. Definitions and examples are given for each word. In addition, an often used device, or "Memory Jogger," is provided you for each word as a guide to aid you in remembering the right word to use.

For example, in deciding whether to use *affect* or *effect*, the Memory Jogger reminds you that the words *effect, entrance,* and *exit* all start with the letter "E." *Effect* means either to *cause* (entrance) or *result from* (exit). If we wanted to use the word meaning "to influence" we would not use *effect*, but *affect*.

How many times have you seen the phrase "held in abeyance" or "afford an opportunity" or 101 other hackneyed words and phrases that have been used over and over again in modern business correspondence? Too many times, no doubt, and you probably whispered to yourself, "I hope I don't use those expressions!"

Figure 3 is a compendium of about 200 words and/or phrases that have been used so often they should more accurately be described as "retreads." You will find by using it daily you will soon develop a knack for sharp, lively, and fresh business terminology which will certainly be a most welcome change. Before long, people will say, "That —— has certainly developed into a good writer!" as *they* continue to use old cliches.

Figure 2

GUIDE TO PROPER USE OF 60
MOST COMMONLY MISUSED WORDS

Affect	**Effect**
Verb meaning to influence.	Noun meaning result or verb meaning to cause or bring about.

Examples: His illness should not *affect* his game today.
Antibiotics should *effect* a cure.

Memory Jogger: *Effect, entrance,* and *exit* begin with "E". *Effect* means to cause or result from, like *entrance* and *exit.*

All Right	**Alright**
Two words meaning completely correct or acceptable.	Colloquialism not generally accepted today.

Examples: Everything was *all right* when I left.
It was *all right* with Mr. Smith.

Memory Jogger: *Complete* and *correct* are *two* words, and it takes *two* words to say *all right.*

All Together	**Altogether**
Means assembled into one group.	Means completely or entirely.

Examples: We were *all together* in the gymnasium.
He was *altogether* mistaken in his opinion.

Memory Jogger: *All* and *together* are *two* words, and it takes *two* or more to assemble or congregate in a group.

All Ready

Two words meaning everything is in order.

Already

Adverb meaning previously or prior to a specified time.

Examples: The Queen Mary is *all ready* to sail.
The ship has *already* left the port.

Memory Jogger: *All ready* means "completely set." *Already* has only one L, which implies that one L (or time) has gone.

Among

Word used with *three* or more persons or things.

Between

Word used to differentiate between *two* people or things.

Examples: Jane is *among* our best neighbors.
Final selection is *between* Joe and Bob.

Memory Jogger: *Between* starts with letter "B" (2nd letter of alphabet); *between* involves 2 things. *Among* involves more than two.

Amount

Used in reference to money or things that can't be counted.

Number

Refers to items that can be counted; a specific amount.

Examples: The *amount* you pay is greater than you think.
Next year, the *number* of plants will be increased.

Memory Jogger: *Number* (5, 10, 20) is a specific thing. *Amount* is not. *Amount* also contains the letter "U," standing for *unknown.*

Anyone

Word used if *any* is important and is to be emphasized.

Any One

Used to refer to some specific person, place or thing.

Examples: I told him *anyone* is eligible.
You may choose *any one* of our floor models.

Memory Jogger: In *any one*, the *one* stands alone and is accented. The word *anyone* is non-specific.

Anxious

More serious. Shows great worry or concern.

Eager

Adjective meaning excited or impatient.

Examples: John was *anxious* to hear from his wife.
Richard was *eager* to bowl in our tournament.

Memory   *Anxious* contains an "X" (usually marks the "spot" where the
Jogger: trouble is). *Eager* is like *Easy* and that's not bad.

Balance   **Remainder**

Strictly speaking, the difference   Used to denote something left
  between debits and credits.   over in any situation.

Examples: The *balance* of your account is $150.00.
            I won't see him for the *remainder* of the year.

Memory   *Balance* usually implies "scales," or something having *two* sides.
Jogger: The heavier side (left or right) will be lower.

Complement   **Compliment**

Means to complete, is fitting, or   Means to flatter or offer words
  add a finishing touch.   of praise to someone.

Examples: The matching drapes will *complement* the furniture.
            Henry was *complimented* for his high score.

Memory   *Complement* and *complete* both have two "Es." *Compliment*
Jogger: has an "I," which signifies an *I*ndividual (recg. compliment).

Continual   **Continuous**

Used to show expected and con-   Used to show constant activity
  tinuing, but stop-and-go   with no letup.
  activity.

Examples: This electric typewriter has given *continual* service.
            The traffic on Highway 80 is *continuous.*

Memory   *Continual* contains an "L" which implies occasional *L*apses.
Jogger: *Continuous* contains 2 "Us" which means *U*nbroken service.

Credible   **Creditable**

Means "capable of being true or   Means performance worthy of
  believable."   credit or special mention.

Examples: The witness related a *credible* experience.
            Liza gave a *creditable* performance.

Memory   Credible contains the word "edible," which implies you can
Jogger: "swallow the story."

Each Other   **One Another**

Used when only two persons are   Used when three or more
  involved.   persons are involved.

Examples: Henry and Sam gave *each other* ties for Christmas.
The machinists were competing with one *another.*

Memory *Each* is generally only a *choice* between 2 people or things. *One*
Jogger: *another* implies *one* more (than two).

Eminent

Means famous or noteworthy.

Imminent

Something expected to happen soon.

Examples: Henry Blackstone was an *eminent* attorney.
The judge's ruling on the case is *imminent.*

Memory *Imminent* and *impending* both contain the letters "IM" and
Jogger: mean the same thing. *Eminent* and *excel* both start with "E".

Enthused

Colloquialism not generally accepted in modern usage.

Enthusiastic

Filled with ardor, excitement or zeal.

Examples: Julia is *enthusiastic* about her work.
Many customers are *enthusiastic* about this detergent.

Memory Saying the extra syllables contained in the longer word *enthu-*
Jogger: *siastic* reflects a greater measure of excitement.

Except

Means to exclude from a group or single out.

Accept

Means to receive what may be offered or to assent.

Examples: Mr. Miller has held all positions *except* supervisor.
Mr. Miller will probably *accept* the position.

Memory *Except* contains an "X" and X usually "marks the spot" which
Jogger: is not included in any set of conditions.

Factious

Adjective meaning inclined to forming factions or groups.

Fractious

Adjective meaning quarrelsome or irritable.

Examples: The Socialist Party is a *factious* organization.
Mario was a *fractious* individual.

Memory *Fractious* contains an "R" which stands for *Rebellious. Fac-*
Jogger: *tious* and *factions* are practically the same spelling.

Farther

Used when referring to specific distance.

Further

Used to indicate extent or degree.

Examples: Gene can run *farther* than 5 miles.
We should give this *further* consideration.

Memory Jogger: *Farther* and distance both contain "*A*s." *Further* contains a "U" (for *U*nknown) which more closely applies to *further*.

Infer

Objectively draw a conclusion.

Imply

Means to hint or suggest.

Examples: You *infer* that these two models are both the same price.
George *implied* he would lower his price.

Memory Jogger: Infer ends with letter "R" which stands for *R*esult (draw a conclusion).

Latest

Refers to the last condition that is still in effect.

Last

Refers to final things—after all others.

Examples: The Fury is the *latest* model we have on hand.
This is the *last* car for sale at that price.

Memory Jogger: *Last* is absolute. *Latest* is usually tentative and something else may supersede it.

Less

Mainly refers to things which are hard to count.

Fewer

Generally refers to people or things that can be counted.

Examples: Jim relies *less* on his own ability than his personality.
We have *fewer* machine tools than the Bayer Tool Co.

Memory Jogger: *Less* is part of the expression "more or less," which is indefinite. *Fewer* starts with "F" which stands for *F*inite.

Lie

Usually means to rest and does not take an object.

Lay

Means to put or place and usually takes an object.

Examples: "Lucky" will often *lie* on the sofa.
Please *lay* the ledger on Chris' desk.

Memory Jogger: *Lie* and *rest* both contain the letter "E". *Lay* and *place* contain the letter "A".

Party

Group of people (except legally).

Person

Refers to an individual.

Examples: John was in the first *party* that visited the plant.
We need a younger *person* to fill that job.

Memory   *Person* also contains the word "son," which generally pertains
Jogger: to an individual. *Party* suggests a group.

Practical   ## Practicable

Adjective meaning useful or   Applies to what has been pro-
pragmatic.   posed but has not yet been
                                       tested.

Examples: George impresses me as a *practical* person.
Jim's idea seems like a *practicable* solution.

Memory   *Practical* contains the word "cal," which may be a man's
Jogger: nickname (person). *Practicable* never refers to a person.

Precede   ## Proceed

Means to "go before."   Means to "go ahead" or "move
                                       forward."

Examples: Cloudy elements usually *precede* bad weather.
After he receives the report, Hank can *proceed.*

Memory   *Precede* contains the prefix *pre,* which literally means *before.*
Jogger:

Principal   ## Principle

Means main or primary   Rule or underlying tenet.
participant.

Examples: Too much talk was my *principal* objection.
Jack didn't care for my "Let the buyer beware" *principle.*

Memory   *Principal* ends in "pal," which could stand for Primary and
Jogger: Leading. *Principle* and *rule* both end in "LE."

Raise   ## Rise

Means to lift up or cause some-   Takes on the more subjunctive
thing to move up.   sense of "to go up" or "come
                                       up."

Examples: This news will *raise* a few eyebrows today.
Carl does not expect costs to *rise* this month.

Memory   *Raise* contains the letter "A," which stands for Active. *Raise* is
Jogger: generally used in a more active sense (urge, lift).

Stationary	**Stationery**
Means situated in one place or without movement.	Paper used for writing.

Examples: You must have at least one *stationary* dock.
Write this letter on our best *stationery*.

Memory Jogger: *Stationary* contains the letters s-t-a-y, (and no "E,") which implies "remain in one place." *Stationery* and *write* both have an "E."

Very	**Real**
Adverb meaning to a high degree.	Adjective meaning truly, actual or fundamental (use with nouns).

Examples: Sam is a *very* successful salesman.
Helen has been a *real* supporter for this program.

Memory Jogger: *Very, exceedingly, excessively* all contain a "Y" and mean "a high degree." *Real* and *actual* both contain an "A."

Without	**Unless**
Preposition used to indicate the absence of something or someone.	Conjunction indicating an exception to the stated condition.

Examples: We will have to proceed *without* Mr. Hart.
We cannot continue this policy *unless* the public agrees.

Memory Jogger: *Without* contains the word *out,* which indicates something is "out" (not included). *Unless* contains the word *less,* which implies something is not complete.

Figure 3

USED WORD LIST

(Old, tired, run-down words looking for a home)

Abeyance. *Held in abeyance* is a pompous phrase. *Wait* and *postpone action* are more natural expressions.

About. *He will arrive at about nine o'clock* is not a correct sentence. Use *at* or *about,* but not both.

Above should not be used in the sense of *more than. His wages are more than* (not above) $10,000 *a year.*

Accompanied by. The preposition *with* is usually better, as his *letter with* (instead of *accompanied by*) *the application.*

Accomplished may be expressed as *done.*

Accumulate. *Gather* is a good plain word to replace this one.

Acquaint. Instead of *acquainting* your readers with facts, *tell or inform* them.

Additional. Vary the use of this overworked adjective. Use *added.*

Advise. *Tell, inform,* and *say* are fresher words for letters. *You are advised* is a useless phrase in any letter.

Affect, Effect. *Affect* is always a verb meaning to modify or influence. *Effect* may be noun or verb. As a verb it means to accomplish or bring about; as a noun, outcome or result. Both *affect* and *effect* are overworked, correctly and incorrectly.

Afford an opportunity. *Allow* is suggested as a replacement for this overworked phrase.

All-around is not correct. Use *all-round.*

All of. Say *all the workers,* not *all of the workers.*

All ready, Already. The first is an adjective phrase, correctly used in this sentence: *When the hour came, they were all ready.* The second is an adverb that oftener than not should be omitted: *We have (already) written a letter.*

Alternative, Choice. *Alternative* refers to two only; *choice,* to two or more. Since there is only one alternative to another, don't say *the only other alternative:* simply say *the alternative.*

Ameliorate. Why is this big word so popular? It's a good word, but so is the commoner word *improve.*

Amount, Number are often used loosely. An *amount* is a sum total; *number,* as a noun, refers to collective units. You have *an amount of money,* and *a number of errors.*

Anticipate means to foresee or prevent by prior action. Don't use it when you actually mean *expect.*

Anxious is proper only when anxiety actually exists. We are *eager* to write good letters, not *anxious.*

Any. Don't follow superlatives with *any,* as *Lincoln's letters are the best of any.* When used in a comparative statement, *any* must be followed by *other,* as *that letter is better than any other he has written.*

Any place is not good usage. *Say anywhere.*

Appear. A woman *appears* to be young, but she *seems* to be intelligent. *Appear* usually suggests that which is visible.

Appreciate your informing us is a clumsy phrase that can be replaced with a simpler one, as *please write us* or *please tell us.*

Approximately is overworked. Why not say *about?*

Apparently. This is a "hedger" to be avoided.

Apt. Don't use this word when you mean *likely. Apt* suggests predisposition. *A tactless person is apt to write a blunt letter,* but *delayed replies are likely* (not apt) *to damage public relations.*

Around. *Around ten dollars* is incorrect. Say *about ten dollars.*

Ascertain is a big word often used when the little word *learn* is better. Don't use *ascertain* unless you want to put over the idea of effort in getting facts.

Assistance. Let's have more *help* and *aid,* and less *assistance.*

At—
  —All Times. Say *always.*
  —This Time. Say *now.*
  —The Present Time. Say *now.*
  —An Early Date. Won't *soon* do?
  —Your Earliest Convenience. Do you mean this? A convenient time may not come.
  —The Earliest Possible Moment. This may be the moment the letter arrives.

Attached—
  —Please Find
  —Hereto   Worn out letter language. *Attached* is adequate.
  —Herewith

Attention is invited or *attention is called* should be needless. If a sentence doesn't make its point without these emphatics it needs rewriting.

Balance. You may have a *balance* on an account, but that which is left after something is taken away is a *remainder,* as *the remainder of the year, the remainder of the office force.*

Basis. Instead of saying *as a basis for,* simply say *for.*

Be back in the sense of return is not preferable. Say, *he will return to* (not *be back in) the office Tuesday.*

Between, Among. *Between* properly re-refers to two only. *Among* is used in referring to more than two.

Biannual, Biennial. *Biannual,* like semi-annual, means twice a year. *Biennial* means every two years.

Bimonthly means every two months. Semi-monthly is used to express twice monthly.

Claim. Do not use *claim* as an intransitive verb. *Claim ownership,* but don't *claim to be efficient.*

Cognizance. Avoid this big word both in its legal meaning of *jurisdiction* and in its common meaning of *heed* or *notice.* Instead of saying *under the cognizance of this office,* be specific, as *this office does not audit travel vouchers.* Instead of saying *having cognizance of this fact,* say *aware of this fact.*

Commence. *Begin* or *start* are stout little words that should not be forgotten.

Commitment. How about *promise?*

Communicate, Communication. Avoid these long words by being specific. Instead of *communicate,* use *write, wire,* or *telephone.* Instead of communication, use *letter, telegram, memorandum.*

Compliance, Complies. The phrase *in compliance with your request* is too formal for a friendly letter. It is often not necessary, but, if needed, may be replaced with *as you requested. Meets the requirements* is a good substitute for *complies with requirements.*

Conclude. It is better to *close a letter* than to *conclude* it.

Contribute. What's wrong with *give?*

Consider. Omit the superfluous "as" after this word. *We consider the case closed* (not *as closed*).

Considered opinion. Forget this one.

Considerable. Use this word only as an adjective.

Consummate. You really like big words if you use this one in the sense of *complete* or *bring about.*

Continously, Continually. The first word means *without interruption;* the second, *intermittently, at frequent intervals.*

Date. Instead of *this date,* say *today.* Instead of *under date of,* say *on of,* or *dated.*

Demonstrates. *Shows* is a good plain word to substitute for this one.

Desire. *If you wish* or *if you want* is usually better than *if you desire.*

Determine. Overworked. *Decide* or *find out* may be substituted.

Develop. Don't use this word for *happen, occur, take place.*

Different is superfluous in this sentence: *Six (different) plans were discussed* at the meeting.

Due to the fact that is a roundabout way of saying *because.*

During suggests continuously, throughout. *In (not during) the meeting he brought up* the question of pay raises.

Earliest practicable date. What is a *practicable* date?

Effect, Affect. See Affect.

Effectuate. A pompous way of saying to *bring about*.

Employed is overworked in the sense of *used*.

Employment. *Jobs* and *work* have equal dignity.

Enclosed—
   —Herewith
   —Please Find   *Enclosed* is sufficient.
   —With This Letter

Encounter difficulty is an unnecessary euphemism for *find it hard*, or *have trouble*. Instead of saying *call on our local office* if *you encounter difficulty* in completing your application, why not say call on our local office *if you need help* etc.? Or, if *difficulty* must be your word, why not replace *encounter* with *meet?*

Endeavor to ascertain, high-sounding phrase though it is, simply means *try to find out.*

Equivalent is seldom better than *equal.*

Event is not to be used for *incident, affair,* and *happening,* unless the occurrence is particularly noteworthy.

Exercise care is a stuffy way of saying *please be careful.*

Expiration. *End* is just as final.

Expedite is a popular Government word. Can't we say *hasten* or *hurry?* Do you know that the Latin from which expedite derives means "to free one caught by the foot"?

Experience has indicated that. Try *we (I) learned.*

Facilitate is another popular Government word. It means *make easy,* but it *makes hard reading* for some people.

Farther, Further. Farther indicates distance; further denotes quantity or degree. You go *farther* away; you hear nothing *further.*

Favor. Does anybody nowadays use *favor* in the sense of a letter? Don't— It's old fashioned.

Few, Less. *Few* is for number; *Less* is for quantities or amounts. *Write fewer pages* and *say less.*

First is both an adjective and an adverb. Don't say *firstly.*

Following. *He retired after* (not *following*) an outstanding career.

Finalize, finalization. These are manufactured words. Why manufacture such words when you have *end, conclude,* and *complete?*

For—
　　—Your Information. Superfluous.
　　—The Month of July. For *July*
　　—The Reason That. *Since, because, as.*

Forward is often used when *send* is better.

Fullest possible extent. A meaningless padding.

Furnish is often used when *give* is better. *Please give (not furnish) us* the information.

Further. See Farther.

If—
　　—Doubt is Entertained. Say *if doubtful.*
　　—It is Deemed Satisfactory. Say *if satisfactory.*

Implement. Say *carry out.*

In—
　　—Compliance With Your Request. Say *as requested.*
　　—Addition To. Say *besides.*
　　—A Satisfactory Manner. Say *satisfactorily.*
　　—The Near Future. Say *soon.*
　　—The Event That. Say *if.*
　　—The Amount Of. Say *for.*
　　—The Meantime. Say *meantime* or *meanwhile.*
　　—Order To. Say *to.*
　　—Regard To. Say *about.*
　　—View Of The Fact That. Say *as.*
　　—A Position To. Say we *cannot* rather than we *are not in a position to.*

Inadvertency. *Errors* and *mistakes* are not glossed over by this euphemism.

Inasmuch as. *As, since,* and *because* are a lot shorter.

Indicate is overworked, but *show* is a stout little word.

Informed. *You are informed* should be a useless phrase in any letter.

Initial is overworked, but *first* is not used enough.

Initiate is a Government favorite for which *begin* is synonymous. Sometimes the word can be omitted, as in the phrase *initiate a citation* (cite).

Incapacitated. Why not *unable* to work?

Insure. *In order to insure* is a common phrase in Government letters. *Make sure* is simpler and more natural.

Interpose no objection. Be direct. Say *I do not object* or *I approve.*

Jurisdiction. See Cognizance.

Kindly should not be used for please. *Please reply,* not *kindly reply.*

Last and Latest are not interchangeable. *Last* means final; *Latest,* most recent. *The last page* of a book, but *the latest book* on the market.

Least is used when more than two persons or things have been mentioned. Use *less* when only two persons or things have been mentioned; *He is the less* (not *least*) *forceful of the two speakers.*

Lengthy means unduly or tediously long. *Lengthy* may describe some of our letters, but *long* is usually the word.

Less. See Few and Least.

Like. Never use *like* to introduce a subject and its verb. *He wrote as* (not *like*) *he spoke.*

Loan is not desirable as a verb. Use *lend.*

Locality. Don't overlook the little word *place.*

Locate. You *find* (not *locate*) a file.

Makes provision for. Try using *does,* or *provides.*

Meets with our approval is a roundabout way of saying *we approve.*

Modification. *Change* will usually take the place of this one.

Near is incorrectly used in this sentence: *There is not near enough.* Use *nearly.*

Necessary is used when *need* would do. For example, you may shorten *it is not necessary for you* to *you need not.*

Nominal means *in name,* and by implication *small.* Why not say *small?*

None as a subject is usually plural unless a singular subject is clearly indicated. *None of the jobs are open. None of the work is done.*

Notwithstanding the fact that is the longwinded way of saying *although* or *even though.*

Objective can be *aim.*

Obligate can be *bind.*

Obligation can be *debt.*

On is superfluous in stating days and dates. *He arrived Tuesday,* not *on Tuesday.*

Optimum is Latin for *best.* Let's stick to English.

Out is superfluous in phrases like *start out* and *lose out. He started* (not *started out*) as a messenger.

Over should be avoided when you mean *more than* in referring to a number. *There were more than* (not *over*) *five hundred* people at the meeting.

Over the signature of is an unnatural way of saying *signed by.*

Pamphlet need not be described as *little*. The suffix *let* on words like booklet, leaflet, and hamlet, means *little* or *small.*

Past. Say *last year*, not *past year*, if you mean the preceding year.

Part. *Our error* is better than *an error on our part.*

Participate is a common word, but *take part* is a good plain way of saying the same thing.

Party. Does anyone use this for *person* any more? Don't.

Pecuniarily interested. Like so many of our pompous phrases, this one originated to cover a broad meaning. Substitutes for phrases like these do not always satisfy our legal advisers. But you might try *financial interest* or *interest in profit.*

Per need not be used for our English article "a." Avoid the Latin terms, *per annum, per diem,* and so on. Say *a year* and *a day.*

Photostatic copies. *Photostats* is a word now generally accepted.

Place. See Any Place.

Portion. *Part of the time,* not *portion* of the time.

Possess. Why not *have?*

Practically is overworked. Use *virtually, almost, nearly.*

Preclude. Do you use this word whenever you can work it in? Vary your usage with *shut out* or *prevent.* Many letterwriters overwork the phrase *preclude the necessity.*

Predecease is often used as a euphemism. Euphemisms are not as tone-invoking as you may think. Say *die before.*

Predicated on the assumption. Forget this one.

Preventive is better than the irregular doublet *preventative.*

Previous to, Prior to. Why not *before?*

Principal, Principle. The noun *principal* means head or chief, as well as capital sum. The adjective *principal* means highest or best in rank or importance. *Principle* means truth, belief, policy, conviction, or general theory.

Process of preparation doesn't make the action any more important than *being prepared* or *we are preparing.*

Procure. Some people say this is the common Government word for *get.*

Proven should not be used as the past participle of *prove.* Use *proved. Proven* may be used as an adjective.

Promulgate. A long word for *issue.*

Providing should not be used for *if* or *provided*. *Providing* low-cost houses is a problem but we will meet the problem *provided* the builders get supplies.

Pursuant to. *Under* will usually take the place of this one.

Quite means *really, truly, wholly, positively.* Avoid its use in phrases like *quite a few* and *quite some*.

Rarely ever, Seldom ever. *Ever* is superfluous in phrases like these. Say *we seldom fail,* not *we seldom ever fail.*

Recent date is meaningless. Either give the date of the letter or omit any reference to it.

Regarding is overworked. Little words wear better, so try using *about* oftener.

Remuneration. Why not *pay?*

Render. Use give in the sense of *giving help.*

Respecting. If you mean *about,* why not say *about?*

Reside. The chances are you seldom use this word in talking. The talk word *live* is the natural one for a letter.

Retain. *Keep* is not a word to shun.

Review of our records indicates. If the information can come only from the record, omit this phrase.

State is more formal than say.

Secure. Avoid this word when *get, take,* or *obtain* is better.

Seldom ever. *Ever* is superfluous.

Some should not be used in the sense of *somewhat, a little, or rather.* His letters are *somewhat* (not *some*) better.

Sort. Never say *these sort* or *those sort.* Say *this sort* or *those sorts.*

Spouse. Unless you are quoting a law, why use this word in preference to *husband* or *wife?*

Still remains. *Still* adds nothing to the meaning of *remains.*

Submitted. *Sent.*

Subsequent to. *After.*

Sufficient. *Enough.*

Terminated. *Ended* may be just as final.

This—
   —Is To Inform You. Omit.
   —Is To Acknowledge and Thank You. *Thank you* is enough.

Transmit. *Send* is better.

Unknown should be avoided in the sense of *unidentified.*

Until such time as. *Until* is enough.

Utilization is an inflated word for *use.*

Verification may be *proof.*

Very is redundant in the phrase *very* complete. *Complete* is absolute.

Visitation. Why should anyone use this word in the place of *visit?*

Wish to apologize, Wish to advise. Instead of the first phrase, simple say we *apologize.* Instead of the second phrase, start off with what you have to say.

It has come to my attention or **It has been brought to my attention** or **It has occurred to me** are certainly time-worn and vacuous phrases. What is this—Judgment Day with you appointed to sit in judgment of the writer? Wouldn't it be better to be a little more human?

13

Researching the
Business Report

One of the hardest problems people face in preparing or writing a report is getting over their distaste for the job. Chances are they didn't ask for the assignment in the first place. Secondly, the job probably came up right "smack dab in the middle" of another project and they naturally resented the intrusion.

This feeling of frustration interferes with our mental processes and, of course, adversely affects the end product. The first thing, therefore, that has to be done to clear the way for effective action is to change our mental attitude.

If your attitude can be slowly changed from hatred or revulsion to tolerance, then acceptance, and finally active interest and involvement, the mind rises to the challenge to see how good a product you can produce. Conversely, if you continue to strongly dislike the task of "paperwork," you are going to try to do as quick a job as you can. If you do this, your research, your preparation, and your report will, of necessity, be inadequate. You will resent the next one even more.

The ability to write effective reports is one of the most useful skills you can acquire. To a large degree, you will be judged by the calibre of reports you write. If you write a poor report, regardless of the reason, you will not impress anyone, especially your boss.

This is where attitude plays an important part. Whether you look upon report writing as drudgery or as an opportunity to "show your stuff," will depend on two things. First, it will depend on how well you can learn the techniques of report writing. Secondly, you will have to visualize and become interested in achieving the *objective* of the report. Once you have done this, you will find your mind is equal to the task.

If your writing isn't clear, the reader won't know what you want him to do. If you don't say what you mean the first time, he has to ask for clarification. If you're wordy, he wastes valuable time getting your message. If your choice of language is unusual, too mechanical, or formal, he loses interest. If your thinking is illogical or biased, he won't buy your answers. Poor writing means a loss of business.

The basic purpose of all writing is to get the message across to the reader. You want your writing to convey *exact* meaning. Your writing will be understandable only when you build in the reader's mind a pattern of thought closely akin to the one in your own. If you forget your reader, you may wind up writing something like:

"The executive officer concept demands that he be a capable manager at all levels as he progresses throughout his career. As the individual progresses and enlarges the scope of his responsibility, his knowledge and understanding must of necessity extend beyond the narrow limitations of his original specialty. However, current career development opportunities do not allow executive officers to become fully qualified to adequately discharge the broad managerial responsibilities as stated above."

What is the writer trying to say? Roughly, something like:

"This company expects the executive officer to be a manager, but it does not necessarily train him how to be one."

The writer preferred, however, to be indirect and wordy. Don't ask me why, but it's unfair to the busy reader to have to take the time to figure it out.

From this and many other illustrations we can draw one major conclusion: Too much of our writing fails to get its message across quickly and easily. It doesn't get the message across because the writer forgets his responsibility to the reader. The reader doesn't get meaning; instead, he gets *gobbledygook.* This catchword means that the writer uses: (i) a hundred words to say what he could just as easily have said in twenty; (ii) words of 3 or 4 syllables when simpler words would do the job; and (iii) several jumbled, unrelated, or illogical ideas.

This failure, you say, is inexcusable, and you're right. It wastes manhours, money, and material. It doesn't get the job done and it seriously interferes with the mission of your organization.

Then what can be done to make your writing simple, clear, and understandable? The following chapters supply some of the solutions to the problem.

WHAT IS A REPORT?

You may well ask this and it is not an easy question to answer. The terminology of industry more often stems from company practice than from any hard and fast set of rules. The best way to define a report, probably, is in terms of what it does. The usefulness of your reports, in the long run, is a major determining factor in how good or bad a report really is.

Business reports cover a wide number of subjects, dealing with all aspects of business activity; therefore, there are many ways of classifying them. Below is what might be called a representative list:

Accounting	Personnel (various types)
Advertising	Policy statements
Annual activity	Product analyses
Attitude surveys	Progress and status
Credit reports	Research
Employee bulletins	Sales
Market surveys	Statistical studies

From the standpoint of form, there are two major types of reports: informal (short) reports and formal (long) reports. The former are written for informal situations, and they seldom exceed five pages.

TYPES OF INFORMAL REPORTS

1. The memorandum report is an internal communication, usually handling routine business, and generally presents data related to a special problem.

2. Bulletins are used for both internal and external communication. They are brief and nearly always include information of more permanent value than memorandums. They are distributed to a significant number of people.

3. Booklets are very much like bulletins, for they serve the same generic function. They should be made attractive and interesting so they will be sure to be read.

4. Short reports are similar to a long, more formal type in both style of presentation and parts used. However, short reports omit many details. Still, most companies prefer to get the job done through short reports.

WHEN FORMAL REPORT?

The formal report should be typed neatly and accurately on good quality paper, together with some form of cover letter, and usually enclosed in a binder. The most common reasons for writing a formal report are:

1. The report is the only tangible proof that an investigation or an analysis has been carried out.
2. From the point of view of management or an outsider, a formal presentation makes a better impression.
3. The report covers a specific, longer than normal, period of time and needs to be distinguished from the ordinary.
4. The results of a smaller, perhaps routine, investigation dictated a more comprehensive investigation be conducted and a more formal report be prepared.

KEY QUESTIONS YOU SHOULD ASK

An important fact to keep in mind: reports are regularly read by people beyond the man to whom they are addressed. So, you should ask yourself two questions:

1. Have I written this report as though it would stop with the man to whom it is submitted?
2. What does the reader need to know and what does he already know?

The reader wants the report to show clearly what is expected of him. He does not like to be left up in the air. A report, then, should answer his questions:

1. What is the subject? The first step is to identify it so that the reader will know at once the subject matter of the report.
2. Why should I be interested? The answer to this question brings the reader into the report by showing how it affects him.
3. What is the story in a nutshell? All the pertinent facts should be stated. Do not shorten the report if you're going to leave out essential information. Consider the previous knowledge the reader has on the subject.
4. What action is recommended? The real purpose of almost any report is to get the reader or someone to do something about the matter discussed. Given the facts, the reader now wants to know if he is

expected to make a decision, approve the action already taken, or simply note the information. He will also want to know the reasoning used to arrive at the conclusions.

5. Who else is interested? Frequently the action you recommend will affect other activities. Be certain your report shows the relationship between these activities and your recommendation.

In the final analysis, the quality of a report depends on two things: the *manner of presentation* and *the substance of what it says.* As we have mentioned already, manner of presentation is reflected in the organization, brevity, clarity, word selection, and overall balance.

VALUE AND TYPES OF RESEARCH

The substance of what you say, however, is equally as important as how you say it. If your message is not based on reliable and factual data, logically arranged and analyzed, and leading to reasonable conclusions, then you have, in truth, failed to accomplish your purpose, the same as if what you say is poorly written.

The next most relevant point to make then is: *be sure of your facts.* It almost goes without saying—most everyone, *before* writing a report, is not in possession of all the facts. That is generally the reason for the report in the first place. Therefore, the basic ingredient of a good report is thorough *research.* If the research is not adequate and your facts are not valid, the report is worth even less than the paper it is written on.

A major phase of research is developing facts and figures to support a decision or a conclusion when, at the outset, you know what the end product or objective is supposed to be. Unfortunately, battle lines are not usually that clearly drawn. Many of our projects would be a great deal simpler if the basic problem was clearly stated in the beginning.

An essential question to ask yourself at the outset—or better yet—the one who assigns you the project, is "What's the problem?" You have to know that before you know in which direction to go. The answer will have a lot to do with both the type of research you will have to do as well as the depth of it.

For example, if your company was considering manufacturing some new or different type of recreation vehicle for today's market and your objective was to find out and recommend a type of recreation vehicle that would supply an established demand at a reasonable price, and return a fair profit, you would be wise to check into most of the following:

1. Similar products being offered.
2. Price range of each, and the equipment included therefor.
3. Getting all the cost information you can (by becoming a potential customer).
4. Talking to recreation vehicle owners and getting their opinions on cost, quality, service, and performance.
5. Finding out from other dealers what sells and why.
6. Getting a "feel" for future potential business from all these conversations with dealers and the public.

This type of activity is termed field research and involves delving into such things as:

- your own experiences.
- reviewing someone's working papers.
- studying case files and company records.
- analyzing questionnaires.
- questioning and discussing the subject with other employees.
- reviewing past reports in the same or a related field.

You are generally faced with such questions as:

- what information must I have or would I like to have?
- what is available and where can I get it?
- how much will it cost?
- will I have to pay for it or will the company?
- how long will it take to get it?
- will it be worth the time and expense?

The primary products of business research are, of course, facts and opinions. It is a good researcher who knows the difference. He must be careful in how he uses and presents opinions.

First, he must know whether the source of the opinion is reliable and qualified. Second, does he exaggerate or distort the truth? Third, if he is reliable, is he defending someone, or does he have an "axe to grind" in this particular situation? Fourth, you have to give proper weight to his education, experience, and general knowledge of the subject in determining how qualified he is.

Conflicting opinions don't destroy your research. You need not be afraid to consider them. Many times, a different opinion has led someone to a different conclusion than he started with and he was glad he had the advantage of it. It may open up many new vistas not previously considered.

What are the various types of research you could pursue and how much time and effort is involved? Let's review some:

1. *Bibliographical research.* Process of using printed materials as sources of information. Ideas may be located in company records, bulletins, and pamphlets, books, newspapers, and various other biographical, historical, and geographical source documents. Specific phrasing of the author can not be copied, however. A summary ordinarily indicates the main idea or point of view of the author but is stated in the language of the researcher.

2. *Pure research.* Undertaken for the main purpose of developing new concepts, hypotheses, and applications. For the most part, highly scientific.

3. *Applied research.* Aims to solve an immediate problem or to find an answer to a question based on existing laws, facts, or records. Most businesses use this type of research.

4. *Market research.* Deals mainly with products, sales, and distribution. Surveys of the public's buying habits leading to product improvement and the development of new products or processes.

5. *Personnel research.* Deals with analyses of employees and their likes and dislikes. Data relevant to employees are important to management.

THREE METHODS OF GATHERING INFORMATION

Data gathered for reports are either primary or secondary, depending on their source. Secondary data are obtained from bibliographical research, government agencies, or company reports. Primary data are gathered directly by the researcher, usually in one of three methods: (a) questionnaires, (b) interviews, or (c) observation.

Before embarking on his research voyage, the investigator should study the project and consider its major and minor objectives, whereupon he can set down his approach or modus operandi. This would involve the following steps:

a. *State the problem.* Gives direction to the investigator's thought processes.

b. *List areas to be covered.* Breaking down the subject into component areas for study shows the researcher what areas need investigating.

c. *Select appropriate research methods.* Jotting down what is known from previous knowledge and what is not known enables researcher to decide what additional data he needs.

d. *Write the proposal.* State what data are needed and the proposed plan for getting them.

Questionnaires are used to obtain information on behavior characteristics, to gather opinions or attitudes and to obtain facts. The advantages of a questionnaire are:

a. Questions can be answered at the convenience of respondent.

b. People usually are more careful in writing out answers.

c. Any bias of an interviewer is eliminated.

d. Specific groups or categories can be polled.

e. Respondent can remain anonymous.

f. Questions can be standardized.

If you intend to make a survey for your research project, it is well to plan the whole undertaking carefully before you send out any of the questionnaires. Make them brief and clear so that they will not take too long to fill out. Since you are asking a favor of anyone from whom you solicit information, it is well to take pains to secure cooperation.

When you send out the questionnaire, carefully explain the reason for making the study. In this way, you will dispel any suspicion about your motives. If you think anyone will still hold back information, ask that the questionnaire be returned without a name. If, on the other hand, you think it is necessary to identify each questionnaire, have the name and address typed at the top of the sheet when it is sent out.

Questions must be absolutely clear. They should allow only *one* interpretation and should mean the same to everybody. This can be accomplished by phrasing them in concrete, specific terms.

If much time and effort are required for each answer, few people will respond. Questions should be arranged in proper sequence to enable a continuous flow of thought from start to finish.

Securing information directly through a conversation with an individual is an *interview.* It allows for a direct exchange of information, and the interviewee's voice, facial expression, gestures, and general behavior all contribute to this exchange.

Interviews may be used to determine objective facts, such as events, conditions, or practices, but they may also be used to gather attitudes, opinions, or emotional reactions.

The interview is frequently better than the questionnaire because the interviewer can:

- usually control the situation.

- interpret questions.

- clear up misunderstandings.

- secure more representative replies.

- receive first-hand impressions, which will help him evaluate his findings.

Generally speaking, there are two kinds of personal interviews—fact-finding and in-depth. In the former, the interviewer is trying to get either objective or subjective information, or both. In the in-depth interview, the interviewer is striving to find out *why* he got a "yes" or "no" answer.

When making a survey the interviewer usually records the answers to his questions as they are given. On the other hand, in some interviews, note-taking might constrict the interview. In this case, the information would be recorded immediately afterwards.

The interviewer must always be impartial. His role is not an easy one, for he must always be on the alert, tactful, and friendly. He should like people, and people should like him. A neatly dressed person who is confident and business-like in his manner and knows when to smile will create a most favorable impression.

He should also be accurate and honest in recording his data. Interviewing is an art which can be developed. The interviewer is also an observer, but he must keep his observations apart from his interpretations. His findings are later recorded, tabulated, and analyzed in accordance with the objectives of the report.

The third technique, *observation*, is a chief source of securing first-hand information, and it is often combined with other methods, especially with the personal interview. More than simply seeing or noticing something, observation in its truest sense is seeing with a purpose.

Basically, there are two kinds of observation—controlled and uncontrolled. In uncontrolled observation, the observer views things as they are. In controlled observation, he selects pertinent data for observations and controls the conditions under which he observes. Controlled observation is experimental research and is commonly used in the scientific laboratory.

Careful planning for observation is just as important as it is for an interview. The observer must have a clear and complete understanding of the problem and of what he is to observe. He must determine not only the main points to look for but also the details.

He should also know which ones to emphasize, which ones to sublimate, and how they should be tied together.

One of the newer techniques used in business today is operations research. It is defined as an organized effort to consider all possible factors, alternatives, as well as their consequences in arriving at a solution.

COMPLETING YOUR RESEARCH

No one can tell you when you are ready to conclude your investigation and start writing. You must make this decision for yourself, and it will require good judgment to make it. You may feel that you are on the verge of a valuable find but also realize that your time is limited.

Coming to conclusions is a crucial stage in your work. There is a temptation to jump to conclusions hastily after finding some of the first valuable data. In checking up on yourself, consider not only the evidence you have, but also the evidence you *do not have.* In other words, "round out" your generalizations by considering negative aspects of the case as well as the positive ones. Look upon your findings with true humility and be honest about their limitations.

It is generally a wise idea to put your notes aside for a day or two and let them "cool off," so to speak. Then, when you go back to them, attack them with a critical point of view. Ask yourself these questions:

1. Do I have all the facts here? Will my boss ask me about something I haven't covered or considered?
2. Has *every* statistic been verified and is it from a reliable source? Has old data been updated?
3. Has every opinion been evaluated in terms of who said it and how valid it might be?
4. Have I followed through and checked out other sources for information that were suggested during the investigation?
5. Can any of my statements be challenged and am I prepared to defend them if need be?
6. Have my suggestions been properly identified as such?

To reiterate a previously made point, the type, manner, and depth of your research is dictated by the objective of your project, as well as its scope and direction. To avoid going off in various directions along the way, it is a good idea to keep reminding yourself as you progress what that objective is. Many times you will find that you will have to go back and make corrections, or verify a fact that you have previously overlooked. In conducting thorough research, be prepared for changing directions.

14

Organizing the Business Report

The question now comes up: "How do I determine what kind of report to write and how do I go about it?" The first step should always be: Organize your material *before* you start.

To examine your findings and conclusions critically, put them in the most orderly form possible. Sort and re-sort your notes and reread them until all the facts fall into a pattern in your mind. Now is the time to (1) state your conclusions, (2) consider limitations of the conclusions, if any, (3) show application of recommendations, and (4) construct the balance of the report to support your recommendations.

Check your conclusions to see that you are drawing all of them from the facts you have collected. A careful, honest check on your findings and conclusions is the best possible preparation for writing.

If you have all the ideas you want to present fitted together in your mind, you will be better able to maintain the continuity of thought that is necessary for successful writing. Remember, successful writing depends on thorough research.

Admittedly, working out the organization of a report and putting it together are difficult steps. By far the easiest approach to this problem is to organize the report to suit the reader's needs. A good starting point is to outline (a) how you developed the information, (b) the results of your investigation, and (c) all your conclusions. Analyze this list from the viewpoint of your reader.

The next step in organizing data is sorting and arranging like data into groups. These data generally fall into four groups: quantitative, qualitative, chronological, and geographical. The purpose of classifying data is to group like with like. The type of data you are working with will usually determine the procedure you use. Following are examples of these classifications:

a. *Quantitative* (arranged into size or volume priority).

Cities with largest population in State of Washington:

Seattle	530,830
Spokane	170,510
Tacoma	154,580
Bellevue	61,100
Everett	53,620

b. *Qualitative* (look for common denominators that enable you to combine topics, rather than assigning priorities).

Report on manpower survey of the XYZ Company:

Organization	Man Years Required
Office of Chief	3
Administrative Branch	5
Sales & Marketing Division	12
Engineering Division	3
Procurement Division	7
Manufacturing Division	15
Total	45

c. *Chronological* (arrange in point of time or in the appropriate sequence of events that lead to a certain conclusion).

Gross sales for past six months–G. Hamilton and Sons:

January, 19 ––	$127,500.00
February	96,000.00
March	130,250.00
April	122,500.00

May	132,750.00
June	138,500.00
Total	$747,500.00

d. *Geographical* (arrange in a significant geographical order or distribution).

Property holdings in five district offices of the Smith Corp.:

Northwest District	$ 1,775,000.00
Southwest District	1,556,500.00
Central District (incl. main office)	5,800,600.00
Northeastern District	11,755,000.00
Southeastern District	3,105,900.00
Total	$23,993,000.00

USE OF INDUCTIVE AND DEDUCTIVE REASONING

You can also arrange facts and ideas by following a pattern of reasoning. *Inductive* reasoning calls for gathering various instances together to point toward a conclusion; in other words, going from the specific to the general. *Deductive* reasoning requires clear statements of premises, recognizing common denominators, and understanding definition and classification. It involves going from the general to the specific.

Quantitative data must first be examined and checked for accuracy and pertinency. Data should also be evaluated for its reliability by statistical procedures. The chief problem in handling data is that you must find the best form in which to present it, and decide what statistical measures will make the data comprehensible. Interpretation requires organization and organization requires interpretation; the two processes are one.

Conclusions are the result of reasoned judgment from interpreting the data, and they make data relevant to the problem at hand. Conclusions, no matter how derived, are tentative until they are tested. They must sound practical and be workable.

After testing tentative conclusions by applying logic and common sense, final conclusions are reached. The conclusions that have been proved can be restated as *final* conclusions. Each conclusion should be checked against the objectives of the report.

Conclusions are the basis for recommendations suggesting action that should be followed and, as such, achieve the purpose of the report. Before the final recommendations are formulated, they should also be tested. The writer wants to be assured his recommendations are logical, workable, and sound.

OUTLINE

After the investigator has organized and thought through his data, he is ready to plan his presentation. An outline serves as a means of organizing material and as a guide for writing the report. Business practice often calls for approval of both preliminary and final outlines by the person authorizing the report before the writer continues with his work.

The major use of the outline is as a guide for organizing and writing the report, although its subject headings guide the reader for easy comprehension and reference. A general outline serves as a guide in organizing material, by indicating general divisions for the report. According to function, there are three main divisions: introduction, presentation and analysis, and conclusions and recommendations.

A *topic* outline is used when the writer is fully aware of the relationship of each point to the whole problem and to all other points. A *sentence* outline states each point in a complete sentence. It may also serve as a topic sentence in writing a paragraph. Sentence outlines are used later as briefs or summaries, whereas a topic outline may be used for subject headings and later converted into a table of contents.

The following example is *topical* in format and specific with respect to the material presented:

Data with regard to contemplated expansion of the Riverdale Instrument Co.:

1. Locations considered and advantages:
   a. Southern California
   b. Northern California
   c. Oregon-Washington
   d. Mexico

2. Skills Inventory:
   a. Present skills available
   b. Skills needed in each area
   c. Skill potential in labor market

3. Materials Requirement:
   a. Hard metals (Supply and anticipated demand)
   b. Rubber, glass, and plastic
   c. Natural resources and other materials
4. Costs of Expansion:
   a. Real estate available—lease or buy
   b. Buildings—lease, buy, or build

   c. Equipment needs
   d. Conversion and relocation costs

The following example is part of a *sentence* outline covering the contemplated expansion of the Freeway Trucking Service:

I. Management feels time is apropos for expanding trucking service.

   A. Current trucks, drivers have reached limit of current territory.

   B. Many new areas and subdivisions have been built in past 5 years in surrounding counties, as well as other parts of the State.

   C. Competitive truck lines offering more service and extended lines to customers.

II. Management wants controlled rather than too-rapid expansion considered, to avoid pitfalls of overcommitment without proper safeguards planned in advance. Survey should be made as to the feasibility and desirability of expanding into following areas:

   A. Five surrounding counties and southern part of State within 500 mile radius; or

   B. Western region, including 7 western states.

III. Advantages and disadvantages should be discussed (in a separate report for each move) which will specifically cover the following points:

   A. Potential size of area, estimated number of customers and related income.

   B. Rolling stock and other equipment required to service.

   C. Number of drivers and number and types of back-up service personnel required.

   D. Regulatory and licensing requirements (city, state, and federal) which may apply to increased scope of operations.

   E. Costs incidental to each of the foregoing.

   F. Recommended time-phasing of each portion if planned move is made.

REMAINING SECTIONS

The introduction presents the necessary background for the reader to understand the report. The presentation and analysis section presents facts and their interpretation to the reader. The conclusions and recommendations section is designed to secure needed action.

A reminder is given here to make sure you retain clarity and coherence in your report, especially if it is long and detailed. You must give the reader your analysis, observations and conclusions at the right moment—anticipating his moment of acceptability, if you will. Remember, he doesn't know all the details about the project that you do. He needs a little help.

A FIVE STEP PLAN FOR ORGANIZING YOUR REPORT

Following is a suggested approach to use in writing your report so it will be reasonably well organized:

1. Plan your time so you won't have to do the whole thing in one day. Nothing is as frustrating or as useless as trying to squeeze it all into a few short hours.

2. Prepare the outline mentioned above, outlining the discussion of each topic in some detail.

3. From this outline, prepare a complete first draft. The object here is to get it all down on paper. Cut and slash later.

4. Put the draft away on a shelf for a day or two. Come back later with a fresh viewpoint, or from the point of view of your reader. You can't do this when the material is fresh in your mind.

5. Revise thoroughly, eliminate, summarize, polish. Ask yourself: How does this motivate the reader to reach *my* conclusions? Eliminate facts or research that proves to be irrevelant, as well as duplications and redundancies.

A management analyst once told me, "The body of a report is no doubt the heart of it but I believe, possibly more important than that, are the beginning and ending. What I really mean to say is you can generally count on the beginning and ending being *read*. If the man who is supposed to read the report is in a hurry, he may only have time to read the first and last page of your report. If you make an impression on him, chances are he will take the time to read the body of the report—later on, if not that day. And that may be important to you."

Having accomplished all the necessary research, organized the material, and prepared the outline, you are almost ready to write. In planning the first draft, keep these important things in mind: the reader's background; his general reading ability; the level of material he can take; the scope of material determined by the reader's needs; and the need to talk directly to him.

COMPONENTS OF A FORMAL REPORT

As mentioned in the previous chapter, there are two major types of reports: formal and informal. Although you might not need to use all parts of a formal report, it is well to know what they include and, therefore, be selective.

Normally, a *formal* report will consist of the following parts or sections, even though one or more of them may be deleted:

Cover. Regardless of its length, every formal report should have a cover. It need not be expensive, but the important point here is eye appeal. The report may be going to a customer.

Title Page. In addition to the title, author's name, and date, the title page should include the name of the person for whom the report was prepared.

Table of Contents. Included in most formal reports, mainly to give the reader the key to the report's contents.

Memo of Instructions. Written by the manager or a superior in the organization to assign or confirm the assignment of a study. Cites the authority for the report and should define the project as clearly and precisely as possible.

Memo of Transmittal. Consists of the writer's personal introduction of the report to the man getting the report.

Synopsis. Generally precedes the introduction. Summarizes and highlights the report in such a manner that the reader gets the "gist" of it without reading further if he chooses.

Introduction. First part of the report proper. Usually contains a statement of purpose and a definition of scope. If the report is based on extensive research, the writer should show what application, if any, he has made of his material. He should also define and explain unfamiliar terms or techniques.

Discussion. Contains the background information and the analysis from which the conclusions are drawn. Should include all the facts and statistical data pertinent to the report.

Summary of Conclusions. Should be used at the end of the discussion when the report is long and full of details. In shorter reports, this section may be replaced by the synopsis.

Recommendations. Writer should clearly spell out what steps or policies he is recommending. If he merely repeats what he has stated in the Summary of Conclusions, he would be better advised to save everybody's time and combine the two sections under the caption: Conclusions and Recommendations.

Appendices or Attachments. This portion is mainly a matter of judgment. If the material is beneficial or necessary to a full understanding of the report, but too bulky, technical, or detailed to incorporate in the body, it should be added as an appendix or attachment. In any event, it should be referenced in the body of the report to show where it belongs.

OTHER TYPES OF REPORTS

In preparing your text, you might want to consider other types of reports, frequently classified according to purpose:

- Problem-determining Report. You are attempting to find the causes underlying the problem, or to find out whether or not a problem really exists.

- Fact-finding Report. You gather and present data in a logical order, without an attempt to draw conclusions.

- Performance Report. You present information on the status of activities or operations.

- Technical Report. You present data on a specialized subject, with or without conclusions.

- Staff Study or Problem-solution Report. You analyze the thought process that lies behind the solution of a particular problem. The problem-solving type of report is important to everybody. You use it daily in various forms, such as in verbal reports, staff studies, letters, operating plans, estimates of the situation, etc.

Remember: Before you can report on a problem, you must first solve it.

TECHNIQUES OF PROBLEM SOLVING

In any problem situation, three elements exist; a problem solver, obstacles, and an objective. There must be one or more persons who are interested in reaching an objective, and there must be one or more obstacles to keep the solver from the objective.

Limit the problem. Restrict it to a manageable size by fixing the who, what, when, where, why, and how of the situation. Eliminate unnecessary elements.

Analyze the whole problem. Do the parts form problems that need separate handling? Or do the parts relate so closely to the whole situation that only one approach is needed? Problem-solving generally consists of five steps:

1. Gather data.
2. List possible solutions.
3. Test possible solutions.
4. Select final solution.
5. Take action.

In actual practice, the steps of problem solving do not always follow a definite and orderly sequence. The steps may overlap and more than one step may be considered at one time. Developments at one step may cause you to reconsider a previous step, or it may cause you to redefine the problem. The steps given above should be considered only as a reminder.

One of the most frequent types of reports encountered in today's complex world is the *technical* report. By far the greatest hindrance to their acceptability is the fact that the writer frequently overlooks the need or finds he is unable to put the technical report into terms the layman reader can understand. Your work on a technical problem is not finished when you find the solution. Your findings are valuable only when others understand and use them!

Many technical groups are guilty of using "shoptalk" much too liberally. If your audience is thoroughly familiar with your brand of "shoptalk," fine but, chances are, the use of loosely defined technical terms may cause difficulty for the reader.

The technical man may write a report which is intended to be read by others of the organization or by other technical men. This type of report is primarily for the record. Emphasis is put on the complete presentation of the facts; their interpretation is left almost entirely to the reader.

Illustrations are always helpful and highly recommended for use in a technical report. You need to know how to plan them and make the most of them. A complex report (which includes almost any technical report) presented without illustrations of any kind tends to become a bewildering mass of words.

The visible evidence of the organization of a report is the headings. They guide the reader rapidly through the report, showing him points where his interest may lie. A study of newspaper headings will give you some good ideas for report headings.

EFFECTIVE USE OF PRELIMINARY AND SUPPLEMENTAL PARTS

After you have written your rough draft and refined the report as much as possible, you still have to complete the package by adding preliminary and/or supplementary parts.

Preliminary sections present reference and informational material which explains and further identifies the report. Supplementary sections follow the report text and include material of a general, bulky, and secondary interest for reference purposes.

Possible preliminary or supplemental sections from which you may choose to incorporate in your report:

The *cover* identifies and protects the report. It should contain the title, author, and completion date.

The *flyleaf,* a blank sheet preceding the title page, is used only when the report is written for a high official or when a very high-quality appearance is desired.

The *title page* is necessary for long reports and those that are retained for future use. It should be complete, accurate, concise, descriptive, and should not contain any unnecessary words.

Copyrighted material is recognized on the back of the title page. Included are the date of the copyright name of the publisher, and a notation similar to "all rights reserved."

The *letter of authorization* establishes authority for and states the terms under which an investigation and a report are to be made. It precedes the investigation and is written by the person requesting the study to the person who is to do the study. Its use is optional.

The *letter of approval* may serve two possible functions. If it is written in answer to the letter of acceptance, it may approve the working plan. If it is written after the report is finished, it approves the final report and may be included as part of it.

The *letter of transmittal,* which forwards the report, is written after the report has been completed and is addressed to the person or group for whom the report has been prepared. Sometimes it is separate from the report and attached outside to the cover or title page. Usually it is part of the bound report.

The *foreword* accomplishes the same purposes as the letter of transmittal or the introduction. It establishes contact with the reader and orients him to the report. For practical purposes, the foreword and the preface are the same. The foreword is usually written by someone *other* than the author, whereas the preface is written by the author and gives him a chance to state his opinion or attitude about the report.

Acknowledgment of assistance of individuals and/or organizations in contributing information and in preparing the report may be included in the letter of transmittal, preface, foreword, introduction, or a separate section.

The *table of contents* is a topical outline of the material contained in a report. It facilitates referral to any section of the report by giving page numbers for each topic. The preliminary and supplemental sections, as well as the divisions of the text, should be listed in the table of contents. Typing the preliminary and supplemental elements in lowercase letters and the headings referring to the divisions of the report text in capital letters distinguishes the two sections.

The *list of tables* is also appropriately called "Table of Charts" or "Table of Illustrations," depending on whether charts, tables, or pictures appear in the report. It follows the table of contents and lists the tables in consecutive order as they appear in the text.

Some form of *summary* should be included in every report. It enables the busy executive to get significant facts without reading the entire report.

Material of general interest, or material too bulky for the text itself, is placed in the supplemental sections of a report. It gives supporting evidence to the material discussed in the text.

The *appendix* is a catchall for all supplementary material which, if placed in the body of a report, might disrupt or delay the reading process. Short reports often do not have appendices. It depends on how the report will be used.

The *bibliography* may be included as part of the appendix or presented as a separate supplemental section. It lists all the printed sources used in preparing the report.

The *index* is prepared after the final typing of the report text and is used only with extensive, complicated, long reports. Arranged alphabetically, the index lists page references to important words, phrases, facts, names, and ideas.

15

Writing and Editing the Business Report

Now that you have finished your investigation, gathered, organized, and analyzed your data, prepared statistical charts, formulated conclusions and recommendations, and outlined your material, you are ready to write. If you have not neglected any of these steps, the report will almost write itself.

Since good report writing is based on effective organization, the first draft should be written to record facts and ideas within the framework of your outline. You should keep before you a picture of your audience as a means by which to evaluate ideas as they occur. It will help to keep all your points in focus, relate them to each other, and add perspective and impact to the material.

Most writers unconsciously carry on a discussion with the reader. You can examine ideas from the other person's point of view and therefore make them more meaningful.

FOUR CARDINAL PRINCIPLES OF POLISHED WRITING

Remember, your main objective is to *communicate* with your reader. If you're not getting your message over, you're wasting your time. In order to get it over, you have to write effectively. To do this, you should use the four cardinal principles of polished writing:

1. *Organize your ideas.* Wherever possible, get the five "Ws" in the first sentence or paragraph—that is, newspaper style. One of the first things a cub reporter is taught is to get the "who-what-when-where and why" in the opening and everything else supports it. If the reader doesn't get that much right away, he goes on to other things (at least mentally). You may not think your report should read like a newspaper, but that really is not the point. You are trying to sell your ideas, your opinions, or your recommendations. You are trying to market a product. If it looks well, is well put together, and bears a professional stamp, it will sell.

2. *Use words that will be understood.* There is an old cliche which says: "If you have to look it up in the dictionary, forget it." Of course, that doesn't mean you should stick with the "dese and dose" but, like many other things, you have to use a little judgment in this area. Don't use an unfamiliar word just to show that you know one. If it fits the exact meaning you intend to convey, that's all right but, usually, there is a better substitute.

3. *Use simple sentences and short, brisk paragraphs.* Don't waste your reader's mental effort by using long, involved sentences. Tell the same facts in shorter, brisk sentences. To avoid monotony, however, sentences should vary to a degree in length and construction. Each sentence should convey one complete thought only. If you find yourself catching your breath when re-reading it, look for another way of expressing the thought. Chances are, there are two or three separate thoughts involved. Paragraph structure should be brisk, cohesive and not over-lengthy.

4. *Mean what you say.* It is repeating somewhat the warning signs described in Chapter 4 but, to refresh your memory, watch out for the following:

   a. "Dead-head" words. Words that take up space and give nothing in return.
   b. "Blunderbuss" terms. Words that scatter their meanings over a wide area.
   c. Use of jargon. Tired, overworked language.
   d. "Smothered" verbs. Action verbs which are buried inside another word.
   e. Indirect phrasing. Use of indefinite nouns and intransitive or passive verbs.
   f. Watch your "fog count" (readability level).

g. Unfamiliar words. Words which your reader will probably have to look up.

h. *Reread.* This is most important. You would be surprised, maybe even shocked, to find out what you said in a moment of haste. You will be glad you went over it.

BASIC PARTS OF A REPORT

Simply speaking, the four basic parts of a report are:

1. *Introduction.* Gives the background information the reader needs to know for proper understanding.

2. *Discussion.* Describes what was done to gather data, and relates the findings by analysis and interpretation.

3. *Conclusions.* Spells out the results of the data and impact of one finding against another.

4. *Recommendations.* Outlines what you suggest be done as a result of your research.

The introduction presents the subject or problem to the reader, gets his attention, and furnishes him with sufficient material concerning the problem to lead to an easy understanding of the rest of the report. The findings and recommendations should follow in a logical and orderly sequence.

In many circles today, a report may begin with either conclusions or recommendations; following with the findings and their discussion; and ending with a summary, a restatement of the recommendations, or plans for implementing them.

The discussion section presents information and data, analyzes and interprets them. Important and pertinent data should be included in the text and bulky and less important information relegated to the attachments. Emphasis is always on the final objective. The discussion should lead the reader through the same reasoning process the author used to reach his conclusions.

You should not assume the reader agrees with a concept unless it is generally accepted. Simple, straightforward statements of fact are most easily understood.

The final parts of the report contain conclusions and recommendations. Conclusions result from careful analysis and judgment of the data developed and are the basis for the recommendations made. They may be in summary or analysis form. If in summary form, the conclusion section is a recap of the significant points developed in the discussion section. If in analytical form, conclusions are reached through evaluation and interpretation of the data.

Recommendations point to the actions that should be taken. Supported by the conclusions, they are aimed toward accomplishing the object of the report. Like conclusions, recommendations may also be in summary or analysis form.

Generally speaking, recommendations are presented last, but they do not always appear at the end. They may be given first but, if the reader is likely to react unfavorably to a recommendation, then it should be given last—the report can prepare him for it.

REVISING AND EDITING

Ordinarily, the first draft of a report is written in rapid fashion. One of the first checks that should be made is to determine whether the report is accurate and complete, and whether its purpose has been accomplished. A second validation should disclose whether the main issues stand out in proper perspective and the minor issues are related.

Finally, you should review the report from the broader perspective of completed staff action. In other words, have I done everything my boss would expect me to do? This review should also be made with a co-worker or a supervisor, depending on your method of operation. Major points of emphasis in this review are:

1. Have the objectives of the review been met?

2. Is the report complete, properly organized, and logically arranged?

3. What overall impression does the report give, including language, grammar, and continuity?

4. Have I checked the accuracy and validity of the statistics and conclusions reached? In this review, verify the accuracy on an adding or calculating machine from the *typed* copy after final editing and typing have been completed.

The purpose of revision is to prepare the report for final typing and distribution. Revision gives you an opportunity to correct or rewrite portions and in general to improve and polish the report—all of which may assure its readership acceptance and resulting action.

Editing is basically the same as revision, for its purpose is to improve the report and check the final copy. Although editing is often done by someone other than the writer, a number of authors edit their own material.

EFFECTIVE USE OF VISUAL AIDS

We should pause a few moments to consider use of *visual aids* in writing a more effective report. One authority has said: "Communication does not refer to verbal, explicit, and internal tranmissions of messages alone. All actions and events have communication aspects. In its broadest perspective, communication occurs whenever an individual assigns significance or meaning to an internal or external stimulus."

Visual aids help to relate information and interpretations which can be easily understood and remembered. They emphasize important facts and figures, add attention and interest, and improve the physical attractiveness of a report.

Visual aids include all forms of graphic presentation of data— tables and charts as well as photographic material. You don't have to be a professional to use visual aids, but you should have sufficient knowledge of the different types to be able to use those which will best portary your ideas and achieve your purpose.

The selection of appropriate visual aids depends upon (a) nature and purpose of the report, (b) the way in which the aid is to be used, (c) data to be presented, and (d) background of the reader or audience.

The reader should only be shown a chart or table containing information which he can quickly and accurately grasp. The questions: "What significant point do I want the chart to explain?" and "Which chart will best explain this point for this purpose?" should be answered.

To be effective a visual aid must:

1. Be clear, interesting, and persuasive;

2. Clarify, illustrate, or emphasize a point;

3. Be attention-getting;

4. Provide a change of pace;

5. Save time; and

6. Be appropriate for the discussion.

Following are the more prevalent and practicable types of visual aids used in business reports:

Table. Presents data systematically arranged in columns and rows. It is a logical way of analyzing and summarizing numerical and other statistical data, and is best used when showing trends, comparisons, and quantities of data. Figure 1 is an example:

Total Road and Street Mileage—Seven Western States

State	Rural	Urban	Surfaced	Total (Rural/Urban)
Arizona	36,689	5,980	21,248	42,669

California	119,170	44,966	120,091	164,136
Colorado	75,004	7,311	50,563	82,315
Nevada	47,793	1,911	16,177	49,704
New Mexico	62,721	4,605	20,119	67,326
Oregon	88,814	6,249	59,846	95,063
Washington	65,148	9,950	62,059	75,098

Figure 1

General Reference Table. Presents detailed information for reference purposes. The special Purpose Table, on the other hand, is selective.

Chart. Presents data in some visualized form other than tabular. Information is drawn or graphed to show relationship at a glance. Charts simplify and clarify facts contained in a report. They reinforce the message, emphasize important points, and impress the reader. A chart contains less detail than a table and usually shows comparisions of only two or three points. Instead of following a tabular arrangement, charts use bars, columns, lines, curves, and other symbols for easy comprehension.

The most popular charts are *Bar Charts,* because they catch the reader's eye and are easily understood (provided they are not overloaded). Bars are used to compare different items of a specified date, compare items in two or three respects, illustrate simple, complete facts, and show relative importance of items. Figure 2 is an example:

Sales of Television Sets by Acme TV—Current Year

Type	Quan	20	40	60	80	100
RCA	82					
Zenith	79					
Motorola	51					
Philco	46					
Magnavox	38					
Gen. Elec.	27					
Other	17					
Total	340					

Figure 2

Line or Curve Chart. Formed by plotting items of data and connecting the points by a line or curve. Plotting is most easily done on graph paper, which is why it is generally called a Graph. Its best use is for depicting continuous processes over a time period. Figure 3 is an example:

Analysis of Purchases—Brown Supply Co.—Past Fiscal Year

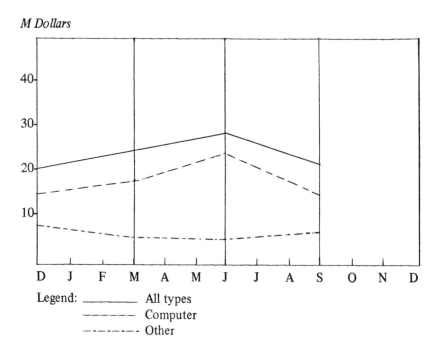

Figure 3

Pie or Circle Chart. Presents data in the form of a circle. The "pie" is divided into segments, usually computed by percentages, and which make comparisons with each other and the whole pie. So-called "Pie" charts can be deceptive, however, and generally should be avoided. Figure 4 is an example:

Distribution of Sales—Home Furniture Co., 19——

Figure 4

Organization Chart. Shows the flow of authority, responsibility, and information among positions in a business firm. This chart (Figure 5) is an organization chart of the Hamilton-Freeman Corp.

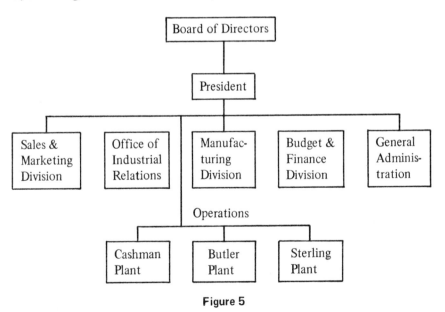

Figure 5

Flow Chart. Used to show the flow of a product or paperwork from the beginning to some definite point, and to clarify the distribution of all copies. Figure 6 is a sample flow chart showing the processing of a sales order:

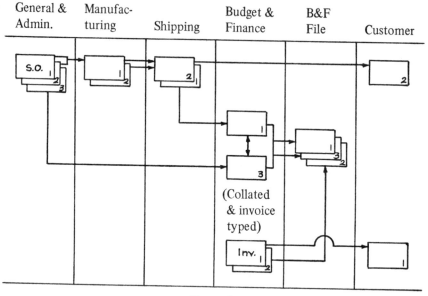

Figure 6

For true effectivity, tables and charts should be as close as possible to the discussion points with which they are related. Large tables should be avoided.

Proper selection of any visual aid is merely the first step in assuring the writer of its effectiveness. It must be appropriately presented in the report and related to the subject. The greater the pertinence, the greater the impact.

DEVELOPING A WRITER'S CHECKLIST

On projects of any size, many writers like to have at their disposal a fairly comprehensive check list of points they want to cover or questions they want to ask. I have found it to be a very handy and convenient tool to use and I recommend it.

Checklists can be developed, of course, for each project. It is usually a good idea to develop your own. There is a more or less general type check list which I have used on a staff study type report and I find it applies to many other types of reports as well. Questions generally asked are:

Problem

1. Is the statement of the problem clear and complete?

2. Is the study limited to a specific manageable problem?

3. Is the statement of the problem free of extraneous and unnecessary material?

Factors bearing on the problem

1. Are the facts genuine? Can they be proved?

2. Are the facts pertinent, acceptable, and authoritative?

3. Should other facts be added?

4. Are facts supported by the attachments, when necessary?

5. Are assumptions logical and acceptable?

6. Are sufficient facts, assumptions, and criteria included to support the possible solutions considered?

7. Are the facts distinguished from assumptions?

8. Are sufficient criteria included to adequately test all possible solutions?

9. Are necessary terms defined?

Discussion

1. Is the discussion concise? Were the attachments used when necessary?

2. Are assumptions and opinions identified in the discussion?

3. Is the discussion developed fully enough to maintain thought sequence without reference to attachments?

4. Are all pertinent possible solutions included in the discussion?

5. Are possible solutions adequately tested?

6. Has the best possible solution(s) been clearly identified?

7. Have attachments consisting of tables, charts, graphs, and summaries been provided to support claims?

8. Is all material contained in the discussion pertinent?

Conclusion

1. Will the conclusion completely satisfy the requirements of the problem?

2. Does the conclusion state briefly the best solution(s)?

3. Does this section contain only material belonging to it? It should not continue the discussion or introduce new material.

Action Recommended

1. Are the recommendations clearly and logically supported by the rest of the study?

2. Are these the most suitable, feasible, and acceptable courses of action to follow?

3. Are you willing to stake your professional reputation on the actions you recommend?

4. Have all instructions or directives needed for implementing the action been included as attachments?

Attachments

1. Are attachments provided for necessary supporting data? Don't make the mistake of assuming the facts are always obvious.

2. Are the attachments prepared for easy reference?

3. Is reference material adequately identified as to source?

4. Are the attachments pertinent to the problem, or could they be considered as only indirectly related?

5. Is reference to all attachments made in the body of the study? No attachments should be included which are *not*.

Writing Techniques

1. Is the material well organized and does it follow a prescribed form?

2. Is each paragraph concerned with one topic or one phase?

3. Is there smooth transition from one paragraph to another?

4. Are sentences clear, complete, and logical?

5. Are sentences free of involved and awkward construction?

6. Is the language free of excess verbiage, jargon, and unfamiliar abbreviations?

As you can readily see, if you use the above checklist, or one of your own making, on any long and involved report you write, you are going to have a much more clear, understandable, and acceptable report than you otherwise would have. It should be obvious to you what this can mean, not only in terms of reader acceptability but also to your reputation and career advancement.

16

How to Build an Effective Proposal

A proposal is a sales document. Any way you look at it, its primary function is to convince a potential customer you have the necessary capabilities to perform certain work or deliver a quality product in a timely manner and at a reasonable cost.

At first blush, you might not feel you are going to become involved in preparing a proposal for a potential customer. This is entirely possible but, on the other hand, the need might suddenly arise. The surprise you get should not be greater than the challenge or the knowledge required to do the job. Moreover, it certainly would be a feather in your cap if you could show your boss you can do it.

For the purposes of this discussion, therefore, proposals should be classified as (1) solicited and (2) unsolicited. The reason for this distinction is the fact that the approaches are completely different. Since the format, style, and technique is more simple and direct, a general outline of the most important points to be considered in an unsolicited proposal will be first.

DEVELOPING UNSOLICITED PROPOSALS

1. Subject and purpose: A brief, definitive, and clear statement of the subject matter of the proposal should be given, as well as the purpose it will serve or what it will accomplish.

2. Refer to previous contacts: If you or someone in your company has had a discussion or an earlier association with the customer regarding the subject matter, comment should be included with specific references to names, dates, and places.

3. Define the problem: Define, in clear and succinct terms, what the problem is all about and how it ties in with the subject.

4. Background: Furnish comments, in sufficient amount to give the reader a more adequate understanding, pertaining to the events or factors leading to or causing the problem.

5. Need for solution: Outline in convincing language the need, from the reader's point of view, for a timely and perhaps money-saving solution to the problem.

6. Benefits: Clearly point out benefits which should or will result from the solution you propose. Emphasize or highlight major advantages of the proposal. Try to personalize and tailor the advantages to the customer. If possible, relate the advantages in terms of dollar savings or future business or profits.

7. Feasibility: Discuss and prove to the customer that your proposal is feasible from a physical, monetary, and a sociological point of view.

8. Scope: Set reasonable limits on the problem as well as the solution. Show other benefits or advantages that will derive from the solution. Be specific in defining objectives of your proposal; material, economic, and financial.

9. Methods to be used: Describe, to the depth and extent necessary for full and adequate treatment, the methods and procedures you propose to use to reach your stated objectives. This step is also supported further by steps 12, 13, and 14.

10. Task breakdown: Provide an identification of the various tasks that will be required to perform the various steps or milestones you have established to arrive at your solution. Tie them together so that there is an orderly progression from one to another and all of them are accounted for.

11. Time and work schedule: Relate the various tasks to a time frame for accomplishment or, as they are usually denoted, to milestones or targets for achieving them.

12. Facilities: Describe, in appropriate detail, facilities which you own or have access to and plan to use in the prosecution of your plan. Don't avoid the question of cost of equipment you do not have but may need to fulfill your project requirements. Outline in some detail any computer services you can furnish and which may materially improve the service you intend to provide to the customer.

13. Previous experience: Essential to cover in comprehensive fashion the amount and type of previous experience you or your company has in direct pursuit of this proposal. This item will be one of your biggest selling points. Stress your performance or degree of succes with similar projects.

14. Personnel: Describe the quantity and quality of personnel who will be utilized in the program plan. Stress the importance of having the right people to do the job, and spell out their responsibilities. State their qualifications and special skills. Outline your personnel policies, e.g., attrition, replacement criteria, reserves to draw on, etc. Discuss employee cooperation or union agreements, as appropriate.

15. References: Provide necessary information to customer concerning previous activities or experience in similar endeavors, with names of individuals who can vouch for you or your company.

16. Likelihood of success: Give the customer ample reason to believe your proposal will succeed. In other words, state the reasons and supporting evidence in such a way as to dispel any doubts he may have that your solution may not work.

17. Products of the project: It is important to point out any other by-products or additional uses of the product which may result if such opportunity presents itself. Many times these added benefits are not easily detected or identified.

18. Costs and savings: Be forthright, accurate, and complete in designating rental or purchase price, as well as any maintenance price after installation of any equipment the customer may have to provide or use. Also to be covered are one-time installation costs; however, the benefits of considering this cost as an investment in future use should be pointed out. In enumerating any cost savings, you are advised to exercise caution and prudence. In other words, don't promise any dollar or labor savings, income or profit increases, unless you are prepared, beyond a reasonable doubt, to prove they are obtainable. Be sure to comment on variable conditions which may affect estimated cost savings.

19. Miscellaneous: This section can be used for relatively minor items, such as method of payment, advertising literature available or which may be used, special terms and conditions related to proposal, etc.

20. Urge to action: Now that the proposed solution or the program has been fully described and all benefits covered, the customer must be motivated to act, or respond in a positive way. Ask for an interview or the order. Try to include some kind of incentive for a quick reply. Of course, this urge to action must be put together in a reasonably neat, attractive, and impressive package to help impel the customer to

respond as you would like him to. This comes under the heading of "effective packaging."

REPLYING TO SOLICITED PROPOSALS

So much for unsolicited proposals. Solicited proposals, or responses to RFPs (Request for Proposals), however, are quite a different matter. The rules for preparing a responsive proposal to an RFP are generally dictated in many respects by the terms of the RFP itself. Nevertheless, the writer of a proposal should be aware of many short cuts to use or pitfalls to avoid in preparing a good, sound document.

One of the most important areas to be aware of in this business is the benefits to be gained in *effective preproposal activities.* These activities many times mean the winning of a job or a lucrative contract which otherwise may have completely escaped you.

Contracts are frequently awarded on the basis of technical dominance in a certain field. More than likely, however, you will be required to engage in a competitive proposal effort. The intention of a Government office or a commercial contractor to issue an RFP is frequently known weeks or months in advance. The most effective preproposal activities, therefore, usually involve *preliminary contact* with the customer.

The main purpose of preproposal activities is to establish communication with the customer to obtain information useful in the preparation of the proposal. Some of the more important areas are:

- Elements or problems disclosed by past experience which will have a bearing on the success or failure of the proposal effort.
- What has been done or what is being done at present in development of the state of the art?
- What factors are used in evaluating the proposal and the relative weighting of these factors? In other words, what is important to the customer?
- Who will evaluate the proposal?

The customer will frequently talk freely before the RFP is issued and he very likely will indicate areas he would like to see investigated. A preliminary analysis of technical capability (by the preparer of the proposal) is a helpful tool in setting up good relations.

Proposal preparation obviously is an important function in getting new business, but good *preproposal* work is also necessary in establishing good customer *relations* and in providing substantive *support* for proposal preparation. For best use of your resources, therefore, a proper balance should be maintained between preproposal work and work in response to an RFP.

Proposal preparation is a critical function in developing new product areas and new customers. It is hard to sell a program to a customer who is not acquainted with your past achievements. A good proposal is very useful in establishing a favorable image with a customer.

It is evident then, even if the proposal is unsuccessful on the job at hand, it may be the basis for a favored position in a future program. Conversely, a mediocre proposal not only does little to win a given RFP, but it can also jeopardize future business prospects.

Most important elements in preparing effective proposals are:

1. Proposal must be well organized for easy assimilation and evaluation.

2. It must be well planned. Proper planning insures coverage of all significant aspects of the problem.

3. Proposal schedules must provide for adequate time for editing, review, and publication of both the technical and nontechnical (cost/management) portions.

4. Proposal must be responsive to the intent of the request, and material must be specific and relevant to the RFP.

Practices and objectives you should follow in preparing your proposals:

1. Write every proposal as if you had to conserve space, reduce reproduction cost, and make it effective.

2. Try to avoid "hard to prove" statements.

3. Tailor background, experience, and personnel resumes to the request.

4. Keep artwork (if used) fresh and relevant and integrate with text where possible.

5. Use varying type sizes to simplify headings and make report more readable.

6. Organize program schedules to show "milestones" represented by performance of various tasks (delivery of material, etc).

7. Arrange tasks in a logical division of work considering relationship to program schedule.

8. If program organization charts are used, show functional responsibility of groups and individuals with time allotted to program.

The above practices and objectives, applied to a detailed, relevant, realistic outline responding to the RFP, can help assure an effective proposal. In the final analysis, however, the total effect upon a potential customer results from a combination of realistic yet imaginative long range planning, good homework (preproposal effort), and effective response to a given RFP. If all three factors are thoroughly and intelligently developed, you can truly expect significant and satisfactory results.

SUMMARY

Before closing, we should review certain basic points. Whether you are writing a long, involved report or simply a memorandum, you should remember the Magic Formula: "SPEED MASON." It reminds you of the key words which, in turn, remind you of the ten most important HOW elements to effective communication:

SOUL

Whether dealing with the public or an employee, or writing a letter, soul encompasses many things. If you desire to be of service, you will have respect for another person's point of view and you will be a good listener. Being sincere inspires confidence, makes for better decisions and more harmonious relationships. When you develop a rapport with your reader or audience, you make him feel important and thus find it much easier to maintain two-way communication.

PLANNING AND PREPARATION

No matter how easy or difficult it might be, planning is necessary and preparation sets the stage for your idea. Having proper knowledge of a research subject, idea, service or prospect creates a favorable impression and an aura in which to communicate. A person must know or understand what *precedes* a subject before he can understand that subject. Adequate knowledge of a subject will almost invariably overcome the natural resistance of the reader. One thing for sure lack of it will most certainly defeat you.

EMOTIONAL STABILITY

Control of your emotions quiets an upset mind, stabilizes conversation, and clears thought processes. It lowers the blood pressure and, since both words and personality communicate, it inspires confidence. It also enables you to think ahead to possible reactions. Being patient, courteous, and tactful will always pay dividends. Good and favorable emotions go a long way towards countering fear, hatred, and suspicion.

EVALUATION

In a changing world, it is not enough to be prepared only to go forth in one direction. Some pundit once observed, "I'm only certain of three things: death, taxes, and changes!" To be ready to evaluate is to be prepared for the unexpected. You must test and measure results of your efforts so that you can re-assess your progress. The knowledge so gained will enable you to intelligently change direction. More often than not, the new direction is more beneficial than the one that was planned.

DIRECTION

The main thing about direction is that it readily identifies objectives, shows priroities, and brings organization to your efforts. It helps your reader follow you down the path to your conclusion which, of course, is what you want. It also helps to influence the indecisive mind and alleviate the pressure of that indecision.

MOTIVATION

Motivation is probably more directly responsible for good communication than any of the other elements. If you are enthusiastic and creating a good image, you will command sympathetic listening to your ideas. If what you say has emotional appeal and gives good reasons for reading, your reader will respond to your call for action. Generally speaking, you must answer a human need and talk in terms of the big "potential," rather than what things appear to be.

ACCEPTABILITY

This element gives the reasons why an idea is logical and reasonable. The idea is given in the jargon or at the level of understanding of the reader. It agrees with (or at least does not disagree with) formerly held or newly acquired ideas of the reader. The person or the idea makes a favorable impression and creates a favorable image in the eye of that reader. Above all, it answers the vital question: what are the objections?

SIMPLICITY

Simplicity makes for better and easier mental understanding as a forerunner to acceptability. It makes objectives crystal clear and puts more sharpness and objectivity into your recommendations. In a training enviroment, it materially improves the learning capability.

ORGANIZATION

When you are truly well organized, you can see what is being done improperly, you can judge what reactions you are going to get, and can tell if you have made your point. You can see how the pieces fit together and how it all affects the end product. Good organization will always go a long way toward putting your argument in its best form and winning acceptance of your ideas.

NOVELTY

Use of the novel approach makes an impression, gains attention, and helps to develop interest. It also helps to maintain interest and counteracts indifference or a total lack of interest. As someone has said, "Before I can talk to my son, I have to wake him up!"

LOOKING FORWARD

We should, of course, look forward as well as backward and consider how these principles will help you in your future endeavours. We have given you the HOW elements for successful writing in all its various forms. You should now have a much greater understanding of the whole field of business communications and you have the tools to work with. How well you apply them is, of course, up to you.